In the Name of Allah, The Merciful, The Compassionate

Can I Ask About Islaam?

A guide for young Muslims based upon the Qur'aan, the Sunnah and the doctrine of the early generation of believers

Book One
The Pillars of Faith

By Abu Omar Faheem Hasan

Straight Path Books
Islamic Publishing
London, England

Published by Straight Path Books Islamic Publishing
137 Tooting Bec Road, London, SW17 8BW, United Kingdom
Tel / Fax : ++44 (0)20- 8672 4799
E-mail : straightpathbooks@hotmail.com

Typesetting & Cover Design ~ Straight Path Books
Cover art finishing by Partners in Print

Cover Photograph of Sultan Omar Ali Saifuddin Mosque, Brunei, taken by Pete Crockford

Printed by Partners in Print
95 Pritchett Street
Birmingham, B6 4ES
England
Tel : ++44 (0)121-359 0202
Fax : ++44 (0)121-359 5550

ISBN 0-9541197-0-3

This book is available at most good Islaamic bookstores or directly from Straight Path Books.

Contents

Note from the author

All praise be to Allah, the Most High and peace and blessings be upon His Messenger, and upon the Messenger's family and companions.

Islaamic knowledge is the greatest gift that any parent or community of elders can give their young. It is a gift that ideally should be imparted with kindness, wisdom and in a manner that remains interesting and easy to understand. Most importantly of all, Islaam must be given in a manner which ensures that the basic tenets of the creed, [al aqeedah], are planted soundly and correctly in the minds of all recipients. With so many deviant and false notions of Islaam prevalent today based upon individual or collective whims and fancies, the requirement for authenticity is all the more pressing.

The aim of this series of books [Can I ask about Islaam?] is to present today's discerning young with authentic Islaam, in interesting and engaging modern prose, whilst still remaining within the bounds of the Qur'aan, Sunnah and the aqeedah of its early followers and scholars.

If anything is correct and true in this work, it is from Allah. If anything is incorrect or false, it is from me. I am open to be corrected at all times. I ask Allah's forgiveness if that is the case and His guidance to ensure that this work is as accurate as possible.

The list of people to thank is simply too large to mention. They all know who they are. For their encouragement, support and naseeha feesabilillah, may Allah Subhaan wa Ta'aala reward them all well.

Abu Omar Faheem Hasan
Al Khobar, Saudi Arabia
5 Jumaada 1 1422; 25 July 2001

Bibliography

❖ The Qur'an – Arabic Text With Corresponding English Meaning – Published by Saheeh International and Abul Qasim Publishing House, Jeddah Saudi Arabia;

❖ Sharh Al Aqeedat il Wasitiyah (Fundamental Beliefs of Islam and Rejection of False Concepts of its Opponents) ~ by Sheikh ul Islam Ibn Taimiyah – Published by Dar-us-Salam Publications, Riyadh, Saudi Arabia.

❖ Fundamentals of Tawheed ~ by Abu Ameenah Bilal Phillips – Published by International Islamic Publishing House, Saudi Arabia

❖ Kitaab at Tawheed ~ Imam Muhammad Ibn Abdul Wahab - Published by International Islamic Publishing House, Saudi Arabia;

❖ The Fundamentals of Islamic Creed by Abu Ja'far Ahmed Salamah Al Azadi al Tahawi – Commentary by 'Ali ibn Abi al – 'Izz al Adhur'i ~ Translated by Sayed Iqbal Zaheer and published by World Association of Muslim Youth, Saudi Arabia

❖ The Names and Attributes of Allah, According to the Doctrine of Ahlus Sunnah wal Jama'ah ~ by Shaikh 'Umar Sulaiman Al-Ashqar; Published by Jam'iat Ihyaa' Minhaaj Al Sunnah, Suffolk, England.

❖ An Introduction to the Sciences of the Qur'aan – Abu Ammar Yasir Qhadi - Published by, Al Hidaayah Publishing and Distribution, Birmingham, UK

❖ Ar Raheeq Al Makhtum (The Sealed Nectar) – Safi ur Rahman Al Mubarakpuri, Published by Darussaalam Publishers, Riyadh, Saudi Arabia

❖ Al Qur'aan al Kareem Tafseer Ibn Kathir – Translated in to English - Published by Al Firdous Publications, UK;

❖ Majmoo' Fataawa wa Rasaa'il Fadeelat al-Shaykh Muhammad ibn Saalih al-'Uthaymeen (may Allaah have mercy on him);

❖ Jahannam Wan Naar (Paradise and Hell) ~ by Shaikh 'Umar Sulaiman Al-Ashqar; Published by International Islamic Publishing House, Saudi Arabia.

❖ Paper on Qada wal Qadar by Shaykh Muhammad ibn Saalih al-'Uthaymeen (may Allaah have mercy on him);

INTRODUCTION

The meaning of the word, "Islaam."

In popular speak, Islaam is a religion. By religion, we mean a set of beliefs and principles by which people conduct their lives. In that very simple sense, Islaam is our religion, our faith. In reality however, Islaam is more than that. For you and I and our families who follow Islaam, it is a COMPLETE WAY OF LIFE.

So, Islaam is not just something we undertake only in the *masjid*?

That's right. Islaam does not just govern the way we pray in the *masjid* (mosque) or the way we fast, or the way we perform other acts of *ibaadah* (worship). No. Islaam governs all our affairs. For example, it shows us how we should eat and sleep, how we should conduct business dealings, how we should treat others around us, how we should form our own governments and so on. It tells us how to live our day to day lives both on a personal basis but also on a collective basis within families and within society at large. Again, it is a COMPLETE WAY OF LIFE.

What does the word Islaam mean?

Islaam is an Arabic word. It has two meanings.

1. "Peace." Islaam is the faith of peace and harmony.
2. The other meaning comes from the root verb, *silim*, which means to "Submit to the Will of Allah."

What is the meaning of "SUBMIT"?

To submit means to give your self up, to surrender. "Surrender" and "submit" are common words in everyday usage. For example, if two armies are fighting on a battlefield and one of them thinks they are going to lose, the losing army will put up their hands in "surrender". By doing this what they are saying to the other army is:

- we're not going to fight or resist you anymore,
- we will put down all our weapons,
- take us and do whatever you wish with us,
- but because we have surrendered peacefully to you, please treat us kindly,
- don't harm us,
- we will follow whatever you say,
- we surrender ourselves to you.

So Islaam means to give your self up totally to the Will of Allah?

Yes. To conduct your self in the way that He has commanded. To do all those good actions that he has ordered of us and to keep away from all those evil actions that He has forbidden.

Can't we make our own decisions based on our own will? If we surrender our self to the Will of Allah, does that mean we don't have a will of our own?

Allah says in the Qur'aan that there is no compulsion in religion. He says:

$$\text{لَآ إِكۡرَاهَ فِى ٱلدِّينِ ۖ قَد تَّبَيَّنَ ٱلرُّشۡدُ مِنَ ٱلۡغَيِّ ۚ فَمَن يَكۡفُرۡ بِٱلطَّـٰغُوتِ}$$

$$\text{وَيُؤۡمِنۢ بِٱللَّهِ فَقَدِ ٱسۡتَمۡسَكَ بِٱلۡعُرۡوَةِ ٱلۡوُثۡقَىٰ لَا ٱنفِصَامَ لَهَا ۗ وَٱللَّهُ سَمِيعٌ}$$

$$\text{عَلِيمٌ (٢٥٦)}$$

There shall be no compulsion in (acceptance of) the religion. The right course has become clear from error. So whoever disbelieves in *taghoot*[1], and believes in Allah has grasped the most trustworthy handhold with no break in it. And Allah is Hearing and Knowing. (Soorah al Baqarah; 2:256)

You can do whatever you like in life. Nobody can force you to do anything. However, if you want to stay within the fold of Islaam, your will or desire to do things must not be contrary to that which Allah wants of you.

For example, imagine you decided everyday at 4 o'clock you wanted to eat a bowl of chocolate ice cream. Could you do it? Would it be OK?

---

[1] False beliefs

10

Yes. I don't see why not because although it is YOUR OWN will, it is an innocent action, which does not go against the WILL OF ALLAH?

That's right. You can do whatever you want so long as it is within the Will of Allah. Now let us say that instead of ice cream everyday at 4 o'clock, you wanted to eat a slice of pork. Could you do that and still say that you are surrendering to the Will of Allah?

No. Although you are exercising your own free will, that will is now against the Will of Allah and so should not be done.

Yes. That's right. You can do anything you like while you are on this planet. However, if you want Allah's pleasure and want to stay within Islaam, you must make sure your will is within the things allowed by Him. If you want to do something that is not in accordance with His will, then you should know that you have disobeyed Allah and will incur His anger. Unless you ask forgiveness of Him and that forgiveness is accepted, you will have to face any resulting punishment either in this world or the next. Remember. Islaam means to SUBMIT to THE WILL OF ALLAH.

Who gave us the name "Islaam?" Did Muhammad sallallahu alayhe wasallam invent this name for his followers?

NO. Allah gave us the word "Islaam" to describe our way of life. Allah says in the Qur'aan:

الْيَوْمَ

أَكْمَلْتُ لَكُمْ دِينَكُمْ وَأَتْمَمْتُ عَلَيْكُمْ نِعْمَتِى وَرَضِيتُ لَكُمُ الْإِسْلَـٰمَ دِينًا

This day have I perfected for you your religion and completed my favour upon you and have approved for you Islaam as religion (Soorah al Ma'idah; 5:3)

What does the word Muslim mean?

A Muslim is a person who follows Islaam, a person who has submitted himself to the Will of Allah. A person who TOTALLY lives his life according to the rules, warnings and advice in The Qur'aan and who follows the practice of His final messenger, Muhammad sallallahu alayhe wasallam.

Does the word Muslim also come from the Qur'aan?

Yes. All the previous Prophets of Allah were men who submitted themselves to the His Will and were therefore Muslims. Allah Subhaan wa Ta'aala says:

$$\text{وَجَـٰهِدُواْ فِى ٱللَّهِ حَقَّ جِهَادِهِۦ هُوَ ٱجۡتَبَىٰكُمۡ وَمَا جَعَلَ عَلَيۡكُمۡ فِى ٱلدِّينِ}$$

$$\text{مِنۡ حَرَجٍ مِّلَّةَ أَبِيكُمۡ إِبۡرَٰهِيمَ هُوَ سَمَّىٰكُمُ ٱلۡمُسۡلِمِينَ مِن قَبۡلُ وَفِى هَـٰذَا}$$

$$\text{لِيَكُونَ ٱلرَّسُولُ شَهِيدًا عَلَيۡكُمۡ وَتَكُونُواْ شُهَدَآءَ عَلَى ٱلنَّاسِ فَأَقِيمُواْ}$$

$$\text{ٱلصَّلَوٰةَ وَءَاتُواْ ٱلزَّكَوٰةَ وَٱعۡتَصِمُواْ بِٱللَّهِ هُوَ مَوۡلَىٰكُمۡ فَنِعۡمَ ٱلۡمَوۡلَىٰ وَنِعۡمَ}$$

$$\text{ٱلنَّصِيرُ ۝}$$

And strive for Allah with the striving due to Him. He has chosen you and has not placed upon you in the religion any difficulty. [It is] the religion of your father Abraham. He [i.e. Allah] named you "Muslims" before [in former scriptures] and in this [revelation]; that the Messenger may be a witness over you and you may be a witness over the people. So establish prayer give regular *zakaah* and hold fast to Allah! He is your Protector; and excellent is the protector, and excellent is the helper. (Soorah al Hajj; 22:78)

$$\text{۞ فَلَمَّآ أَحَسَّ عِيسَىٰ مِنۡهُمُ ٱلۡكُفۡرَ قَالَ مَنۡ أَنصَارِىٓ إِلَى}$$

$$\text{ٱللَّهِ قَالَ ٱلۡحَوَارِيُّونَ نَحۡنُ أَنصَارُ ٱللَّهِ ءَامَنَّا بِٱللَّهِ وَٱشۡهَدۡ بِأَنَّا مُسۡلِمُونَ}$$

But when Jesus felt [persistence in] disbelief from them, he said, "Who are my supporters for [the cause of] Allah?" The disciples said: "We are supporters for Allah. We have believed in Allah and testify that we are Muslims [submitting to Him]". (Soorah Aali 'Imraan; 3:52)

Some non-Muslims call us "Muhammadan" after our Prophet Muhammad sallallahu alayhe wasallam. Is this acceptable?

No. It is not acceptable. If non-Muslims mistakenly use that name, we must politely correct them. We love and respect Muhammad sallallahu alayhe wasallam very, very much. However, he was only a human being whom Allah appointed as His messenger to tell us about Islaam. We cannot glorify, venerate or worship Muhammad sallallahu alayhe wasallam or name our faith after him.

$$\text{مَّا كَانَ مُحَمَّدٌ أَبَآ أَحَدٍ مِّن رِّجَالِكُمۡ وَلَـٰكِن رَّسُولَ ٱللَّهِ وَخَاتَمَ ٱلنَّبِيِّـۧنَ}$$

$$\text{وَكَانَ ٱللَّهُ بِكُلِّ شَىۡءٍ عَلِيمًا ۝}$$

Muhammad is not the father of [any] one of your men, but [he is] the Messenger of Allah and seal [i.e. last] of the prophets. And ever is Allah, of all things, Knowing. (Soorah al Ahzaab; 33:40)

The Christians made this mistake. Esa Ibn Maryam, alayhe salaam (Jesus, the son of Mary, peace be upon him) was sent to them as a messenger. However, they started to worship him and eventually named themselves Christians after him. The focus of our worship is Allah alone and the name of our faith, Islaam, is the name He chose for us, not the name of His messenger.

Give me some examples of doing Allah's Will.

There are many good deeds we can do to show that we have submitted to Allah's Will. For example

- believing deeply in Allah alone
- worshipping Allah alone without associating any partners to him
- being kind and always listening to your parents
- attending to your *salah* (obligatory prayers) regularly and on time
- respecting your elders
- being honest and truthful, being kind, generous and forgiving to others
- giving *zakah* (obligatory alms) and *sadaqah* (charity) to the poor
- always having faith in Allah and looking for ways to make Him happy
- and many more

Similarly, there are things that we can avoid doing which are against Allah's Will

- worshipping others alongside Allah
- missing *salah*
- speaking and behaving badly towards our parents
- telling lies
- talking bad about people behind their backs
- being jealous or envious
- being proud or arrogant
- and many more

What are the main beliefs that a Muslim must hold?

The following is an extract from a *hadith* (saying of Prophet Muhammad sallallahu alayhe wasallam). It relates the angel Jibra'eel's (Gabriel) questioning of the Prophet sallallahu alayhe wasalam and identifies the main beliefs a Muslim must hold.

> Related by Abdullah ibn Omar Ibn Al Khattaab radhiAllaho anho. "He (the inquirer) said: Inform me about *eemaan* (faith). He (the Holy Prophet sallallahu alayhe was sallam) replied: That you affirm your faith in Allah, in His Angels, in His Books, in His Apostles, in the Day of Judgment, and you affirm your faith in the Divine Decree about good and evil. He (the inquirer) said: You have told the truth." (Sahih Muslim)

I counted six things there.

Yes. These are the *Arkaan Al Eemaan* (The Pillars of Faith), to believe in:

- Allah
- His Angels
- His Books
- His Messengers
- The Last Day
- Preordination of good and bad

If I merely believe in those six things, is that enough to consider myself a Muslim?

No. As well as belief, there must be action. According to one *hadith*:

> Narrated by Ibn Umar radhiAllaho anho, Allah's Apostle sallallahu alayhe was sallam said: Islaam is based on (the following) five (principles):
> 1. To testify that none has the right to be worshipped but Allah and Muhammad is Allah's Apostle.
> 2. To offer the *salah* dutifully and perfectly.
> 3. To pay *zakah*
> 4. To perform Haj (pilgrimage to Makkah).
> 5. To observe *siyyaam* (fast) during the month of Ramadhan.
> (Sahih Al Bukhari; Book 1, volume 7)

So, you can see, as well as believing in the *Arkaan Al Eemaan*, without question, we must also undertake the above actions, the so-called *Arkaan Al Islaam* – Pillars of Islaam. For Muslims, belief and action must go hand in hand.

This book is devoted to the subject of the Arkaan Al Eemaan, The Pillars of Faith

CHAPTER ONE

Can I Ask about Allah?

The most important thing to know about Allah is that He is ONE. Belief in this is called *tawheed*. *Tawheed* is the belief in only One God, the creator of all things, worthy alone of all true worship. In its simplest form, it is the belief in the absolute unity of God, absolute belief in the oneness of Allah. *Tawheed* is the most cardinal principle of Islaam, mentioned repeatedly in the Qur'aan and most famously in Soorah al Ikhlaas.

قُلْ هُوَ ٱللَّهُ أَحَدٌ ۝ ٱللَّهُ ٱلصَّمَدُ ۝ لَمْ يَلِدْ وَلَمْ يُولَدْ ۝ وَلَمْ يَكُن لَّهُۥ كُفُوًا أَحَدٌۢ ۝

Say: "He is Allah, [who is] One; Allah the Eternal Refuge; He neither begets nor is born; Nor is there to Him any equivalent. (Soorah al Ikhlaas; 112 in entirety)

Was this "Oneness of Allah" the main message preached by Muhammad sallallahu alayhe was sallam?

Yes. It was the aspect of Islaam he emphasised the most. He devoted the first thirteen years of his *daw'ah* (invitation of others to Islaam)[1] to helping people understand and adhere to *tawheed*. Even before Muhammad sallallahu alayhe was sallam, all the prophets of Allah Ta'aala emphasised to all their people, that Allah is One and only One. For example:

---

[1] i.e. the first thirteen years after the revelation of his prophethood.

أَمۡ كُنتُمۡ شُهَدَآءَ إِذۡ حَضَرَ يَعۡقُوبَ ٱلۡمَوۡتُ إِذۡ قَالَ لِبَنِيهِ مَا

تَعۡبُدُونَ مِنۢ بَعۡدِى قَالُواْ نَعۡبُدُ إِلَٰهَكَ وَإِلَٰهَ ءَابَآئِكَ إِبۡرَٰهِـۧمَ

وَإِسۡمَٰعِيلَ وَإِسۡحَٰقَ إِلَٰهًا وَٰحِدًا وَنَحۡنُ لَهُۥ مُسۡلِمُونَ ﴿١٣٣﴾

Or were you witnesses when death approached Jacob, when he said to his sons: "What will you worship after me?" They said: "We will worship your God and the God of your fathers, Abraham Ishma`el and Isaac - the One God [Allah alone]. And we are Muslims [in submission] to Him." (Soorah al Baqarah; 2:133)

لَقَدۡ أَرۡسَلۡنَا نُوحًا إِلَىٰ قَوۡمِهِۦ فَقَالَ يَٰقَوۡمِ ٱعۡبُدُواْ ٱللَّهَ مَا لَكُم مِّنۡ إِلَٰهٍ

غَيۡرُهُۥٓ إِنِّىٓ أَخَافُ عَلَيۡكُمۡ عَذَابَ يَوۡمٍ عَظِيمٍ ﴿٥٩﴾

We had certainly sent Noah to his people, and he said: "O my people, worship Allah; you have no deity other than Him. Indeed I fear for you the punishment of a tremendous Day! (Soorah al A'raaf; 7:59)

وَٱتَّبَعۡتُ مِلَّةَ ءَابَآءِىٓ إِبۡرَٰهِيمَ وَإِسۡحَٰقَ وَيَعۡقُوبَ مَا كَانَ لَنَآ أَن نُّشۡرِكَ

بِٱللَّهِ مِن شَىۡءٍ ذَٰلِكَ مِن فَضۡلِ ٱللَّهِ عَلَيۡنَا وَعَلَى ٱلنَّاسِ وَلَٰكِنَّ أَكۡثَرَ ٱلنَّاسِ

لَا يَشۡكُرُونَ ﴿٣٨﴾

"And I have followed the religion of my fathers, Abraham, Isaac and Jacob. And it was not for us to associate anything with Allah. That is from the favour of Allah upon us and upon the people, but most of the people are not grateful. (Words of Yoosuf alayhe salaam [Joseph peace be upon him] to his fellow prisoners in Soorah Yoosuf; 12:38)

ثُمَّ أَوۡحَيۡنَآ إِلَيۡكَ أَنِ ٱتَّبِعۡ مِلَّةَ إِبۡرَٰهِيمَ حَنِيفًا وَمَا كَانَ مِنَ ٱلۡمُشۡرِكِينَ

Then We revealed to you, [O Muhammad], to follow the religion of Abraham, inclining toward truth; and he was not of those who associate others with Allah. (Soorah an Nahl; 16:123)

16

So, *tawheed* is very important? What does it involve?

Tawheed can be divided into three main categories:

1.   *Tawheed al Uluhiyyah* (Oneness of the Worship of Allah)
2.   *Tawheed ar Rububiyyah* (Oneness of the Lordship of Allah)
3.   *Tawheed al Asma wa As Siffaat* (Oneness of the Names and Attributes of Allah)

Wow. That sounds complicated. Look, I know Allah is One, do I really have to learn about these categories?

Tawheed is such a critical issue in Islaamic belief, the more you know about it, the better your understanding of Islaam and of Allah.   And anyway, there is *hasanah* (reward) in good knowledge you acquire *feesabilillah* (for the Sake of Allah).

OK. Let's go for it?

CHAPTER TWO

Can I Ask about Tawheed al Uluhiyyah?

Tawheed al Uluhiyyah refers to Unity in Worship. To believe that nothing has the right to be worshipped but Allah. When we pray, we pray only to Allah. We fast only for Allah. We do Haj only for Allah. When we seek His pleasure or His help, we seek it from Him alone and approach Him directly, not through other channels or through go-betweens. All our acts of worship are done for Him alone.

قُــلْ إِنَّ صَلَاتِــى وَنُسُــكِى وَمَحْيَــاىَ وَمَمَــاتِى لِلَّـهِ رَبِّ ٱلْعَــلَمِيـنَ ﴿١٦٢﴾ لَا شَــرِيكَ لَــهُۥ وَبِــذَٰلِكَ أُمِــرْتُ وَأَنَــا أَوَّلُ ٱلْمُسْــلِمِينَ ﴿١٦٣﴾

Say: "Indeed my prayer, my rites of sacrifice, my living and my dying are for Allah, Lord of the Worlds. No partner has He. And this I have been commanded, and I am the first [among you] of the Muslims [i.e. those who submit to the Will of Allah]. (Soorah al An'aam; 6:162-163)

So, nobody can share that worship?

That's right. *Tawheed al Uluhiyyah* is to believe that Allah has absolutely no partners, associates, family etc. Nothing or no one shares the worship and devotion of His creation. All the devotion and *ibaadah* of Allah's creation should be directed only to Him. None has the right to be worshipped but Allah. That very worship was in fact the sole purpose of our creation as humans. Allah Ta'aala says:

$$\text{وَمَا خَلَقْتُ الْجِنَّ وَالْإِنسَ إِلَّا لِيَعْبُدُونِ ۝}$$

And I did not create the *jinn* and mankind except to worship Me. (Soorah adh Dhaariyaat; 51:56)[1]

So, what about people who are worshipping other things than Allah?

They are committing the most serious sin of all, the sin of *shirk*. *Shirk* means to associate partners with Allah. The Arabic word *shirk* itself is derived from the word "partner."

So those people who pray to statue-gods, like Hindus and Buddhists for example, are committing *shirk*?

Yes. They worship mere pieces of stone when, in fact as His creation, their true devotion should be to the one unseen Allah. Those statues can neither harm nor help any one.

What about the Christian who says he believes in one God but prays to Jesus as His son. Has he broken the rule of *Tawheed al Uluhiyyah* and committed *shirk*?

Yes. It is one thing to respect people like Esa ibn Maryam (Jesus, the son of Mary - Alayhumma salaam [peace be upon them both]) and even Maryam, herself, as great and pious servants of Allah. However, it is quite another thing to pray to them alongside any prayers to Allah. That is totally *haraam* (forbidden) and constitutes *shirk*.

Christians may declare their belief in one God. However, the moment they bow in prayer to Jesus alongside God, they have made a mockery of that declaration. They instantly fall outside *Tawheed al Uluhiyyah*, because they have associated someone else with Allah and shared their worship with that person. Allah Ta'aala says:

$$\text{يَٰٓأَهْلَ الْكِتَٰبِ لَا تَغْلُوا۟ فِى دِينِكُمْ وَلَا تَقُولُوا۟ عَلَى اللَّهِ إِلَّا الْحَقَّ ۚ إِنَّمَا الْمَسِيحُ عِيسَى ابْنُ مَرْيَمَ رَسُولُ اللَّهِ وَكَلِمَتُهُۥٓ أَلْقَىٰهَآ إِلَىٰ مَرْيَمَ وَرُوحٌ مِّنْهُ ۖ فَـَٔامِنُوا۟ بِاللَّهِ وَرُسُلِهِۦ ۖ وَلَا تَقُولُوا۟ ثَلَٰثَةٌ ۚ انتَهُوا۟ خَيْرًا لَّكُمْ ۚ إِنَّمَا اللَّهُ إِلَٰهٌ وَٰحِدٌ ۖ سُبْحَٰنَهُۥٓ أَن يَكُونَ لَهُۥ وَلَدٌ ۘ لَّهُۥ مَا فِى السَّمَٰوَٰتِ وَمَا فِى الْأَرْضِ ۗ وَكَفَىٰ بِاللَّهِ وَكِيلًا ۝}$$

---

[1] WA- MAA KHALAQTU AL- JINN WA- AL- 'INS 'ILLAA LI- YAcBUDO -NI

O People of the Scripture, do not commit excess in your religion[1] or say that about Allah except the truth. The Messiah, Jesus, the son of Mary was but a messenger of Allah and His Word which He directed to Mary and a soul [created at a command] from Him. So believe in Allah and His messengers. And do not say, "Three;" Desist: it is better for you. Indeed, Allah is but one God. Exalted is He above having a son. To Him belong whatever is in the heavens and whatever is in the earth. And sufficient is Allah as Disposer of affairs. (Soorah an Nisaa'; 4:171)

Above I asked about Hindus and Christians. It is very clear how they can fall outside *Tawheed al Uluhiyyah*. But what about Muslims? Is it possible for Muslims to break the rules of *tawheed*?

Yes. It happens. Muslims who turn to others for help or plea with them to act as a go-between, between them and Allah are contravening *Tawheed al Uluhiyyah*. Those people who visit so called sages, wise men, peers, murshads and so on, to ask Allah's help on their behalf, are examples of this.

How can these so-called sages ask Allah's help on behalf of others? What makes them so special?

That's right. How do the people who visit these sages know what's in their hearts. Remember. Nobody has the right to stand as an intercessor between a person and Allah except with Allah's permission. Allah reminds us:

مَن ذَا ٱلَّذِى يَشۡفَعُ عِندَهُۥٓ إِلَّا بِإِذۡنِهِۦ

Who is it that can intercede with Him except by His permission? (Soorah al Baqarah 2:255)

Yes. It seems obvious that if someone seeks the help of Allah, they should themselves get on the *sujaada* (prayer mat) or go to the *masjid*.

Yes. They should themselves seek that help directly from Allah. There is no barrier or obstacle between Him and His creation. No one has the power to harm or help you except Allah. He says:

وَلَا تَدۡعُ مِن دُونِ ٱللَّهِ مَا لَا يَنفَعُكَ وَلَا يَضُرُّكَ فَإِن فَعَلۡتَ فَإِنَّكَ إِذًا مِّنَ

ٱلظَّٰلِمِينَ ١٠٦

---

[1] Such as attributing divine qualities to certain creations of Allah or revering them excessively.

And do not invoke besides Allah that which neither benefits you nor harms you, for if you did, then indeed you would be of the wrong doers." (Soorah Yoonus; 10:106)

Does this apply to Muslims who visit the graves of others seeking help?

Yes. It is bizarre that people should ask the "living" for assistance in communicating with Allah Subhaana. It is even more bizarre and, and in fact *haraam*, if people should ask the same of the dead. Allah Subhaana says:

$$وَمَا يَسْتَوِى ٱلْأَحْيَآءُ وَلَا ٱلْأَمْوَٰتُ إِنَّ ٱللَّهَ يُسْمِعُ مَن يَشَآءُ وَمَآ أَنتَ بِمُسْمِعٍ$$

$$مَّن فِى ٱلْقُبُورِ ﴿٢٢﴾$$

And not equal are the living and the dead. Indeed, Allah causes to hear whom He wills, but you cannot make hear those who are in the graves. (Soorah Faatir; 35:22)

According to a *hadith* related by Aisha and Abdullah bin Abas (radhi Allaho Anhumma):

When the last moment of the life of Allah's Apostle (sallallahu alayhe was sallam) came he started putting his 'Khamisa' on his face and when he felt hot and short of breath he took it off his face and said, "May Allah curse the Jews and Christians for they built the places of worship at the graves of their Prophets." The Prophet (sallallahu alayhe was sallam) was warning (Muslims) of what those had done. (Sahih Al Bukhari; vol.1/427)

There is a line in the Qur'aan, in Soorah al Faatihah which reads, "You alone we worship[1]." This seems to be a clear and strong confirmation of *Tawheed al Uluhiyyah*.

Yes. When you express such an intention to worship Allah alone, how can you then associate partners with Him in that worship. But notice something else. You have quoted only half that ayah (verse). Consider the rest of it, (interpretation of the meaning), "You alone we worship and to you alone we ask for Help."(1:5). Again, it's so obvious. It's not just *ibaadah* to others we should be careful of. Relying upon others for help besides Allah can also be *shirk*. These particular lines are not tucked away, hidden in some corner of Allah Subhaan wa Ta'aala's book. They appear right at the beginning of the Qur'aan and with full force. Muslims even utter this declaration in their *salah* many times everyday.

---

[1] Interpretation of the Meaning of the Qur'aan, (1:5)

Before we move on let me turn the question around. What do we mean by *Tawheed al Uluhiyyah*?

To believe that none has the right to be worshipped except Allah.

Good.

CHAPTER THREE

Can I ask about Tawheed Al Rububiyyah?

Tawheed al Rububiyyah involves believing that there is only one Lord of creation, to believe that Allah is the sole creator and sustainer of everything in the universe. He is the sole maintainer of all in His creation. The name *Tawheed al Rububiyyah* is derived from the root word *Rab*, used to describe Allah. Allah is the *Rab* of all creation.

What does the word *Rab* mean?

The word *Rab* is commonly translated as "Lord". Some of the translations more accurately describe *Rab* as sustainer, cherisher or fosterer. It is a word that describes a power who creates something and thereafter maintains it in an extremely careful manner. Allah Subhaan Wa T'aala takes care of His creation without weariness or fatigue, and that's why He is called *Rab*. "Lord" is an acceptable translation and of course is easier to understand. However, whenever you hear the word *Rab*, always bear in mind the above deeper meaning.

Is Allah then the *Rab* of EVERYTHING within the universe or just of humans, or humans and *jinn* or even just of the Muslims?

Allah is one and cannot be many "*Rab*s" to different things. Allah is *Rab* of all His creation. He is the *Rab* of every insect that crawls across the sand, every bird that wings its flight. Animals do not have separate *Rab*s, neither do humans. Whatever the divisions and disagreements amongst man, Allah is the *Rab* of them all, whether they be so called Christian, Jew, Hindu, whatever. It is irrelevant who we think is our *Rab*. Our actual *Rab* is Allah. He is *Rab* of all creation.

أَيُشْرِكُونَ مَا لَا يَخْلُقُ شَيْئًا وَهُمْ يُخْلَقُونَ ۝ وَلَا يَسْتَطِيعُونَ

لَهُمْ نَصْرًا وَلَآ أَنفُسَهُمْ يَنصُرُونَ ۝

Do they associate with Him those who create nothing and they are [themselves] created? And they [i.e. the false deities] are unable to [give] them help nor are they able to help themselves. (Soorah al A'raaf; 7:191-192)

Imagine if there were separate gods, sharing creation and the continual maintenance of everything. What do you think the consequences would be? What if they disagreed over something? What would they do? For example, imagine that if one god want to create something new and the other didn't. How would they settle their dispute?

Well it seems the ultimate alternative is for them to fight it out.

Yes. Can you imagine the scene? Gods fighting over what should or should not be created. What should or should not be destroyed. Who should live, who should die. Over every issue there could be disagreement.

That would be a horrific scenario, especially for us as the creation.

Yes. Imagine if one god decided that the sun shouldn't come up one morning and the other demanded "NO...keep it as it is." What would happen to you and I while they fight it out? No sunshine, no heat, no energy, no food production and so on. The fight itself may result in total destruction. It truly would be horrific.

The sun rising is just one example. I am sure there are so many examples that require Allah's sustenance everyday.

Yes. Allah Subhaan wa Ta'aala says

يَسْـَٔلُهُۥ مَن فِى ٱلسَّمَـٰوَٰتِ وَٱلْأَرْضِ كُلَّ يَوْمٍ هُوَ فِى شَأْنٍ ۝

Whoever is within the heavens and earth asks Him; every day He is in [i.e. bringing about] a matter[1]. (Soorah ar Rahmaan 55:29)

Allah attends to millions and millions of events everyday, without which the universe would not function. These events do not weary him. If He had to deliberate, negotiate, discuss or even fight over these events with another god, *Allahu a'alim* (Allah knows best) the universe may well come to a standstill and even be destroyed altogether. Allah Subhaana says:

---

[1] For each of His creatures

لَوۡ كَانَ فِيهِمَآ ءَالِهَةٌ إِلَّا ٱللَّهُ لَفَسَدَتَا فَسُبۡحَٰنَ ٱللَّهِ رَبِّ ٱلۡعَرۡشِ عَمَّا يَصِفُونَ ۝

Had there been within them [i.e. the heavens and the earth] gods besides Allah, they both would have been ruined. So exalted is Allah, the Lord of the Throne, above what they describe. (Soorah al Anbiyaa' 21:22)

So, Allah created everything alone and controls everything alone?

يُولِجُ ٱلَّيۡلَ فِى ٱلنَّهَارِ وَيُولِجُ ٱلنَّهَارَ فِى ٱلَّيۡلِ وَسَخَّرَ ٱلشَّمۡسَ وَٱلۡقَمَرَ كُلٌّ يَجۡرِى لِأَجَلٍ مُّسَمًّى ذَٰلِكُمُ ٱللَّهُ رَبُّكُمۡ لَهُ ٱلۡمُلۡكُ وَٱلَّذِينَ تَدۡعُونَ مِن دُونِهِۦ مَا يَمۡلِكُونَ مِن قِطۡمِيرٍ ۝ إِن تَدۡعُوهُمۡ لَا يَسۡمَعُوا۟ دُعَآءَكُمۡ وَلَوۡ سَمِعُوا۟ مَا ٱسۡتَجَابُوا۟ لَكُمۡ وَيَوۡمَ ٱلۡقِيَٰمَةِ يَكۡفُرُونَ بِشِرۡكِكُمۡ وَلَا يُنَبِّئُكَ مِثۡلُ خَبِيرٍ ۝

He causes the night to enter the day, and He causes the day to enter the night and has subjected the sun and the moon – each running [its course] for a specified term. That is Allah your Lord, to Him belongs all Sovereignty. And those whom you invoke other than Him do not possess [as much as] the membrane of a date seed.

If you invoke them, they do not hear your supplication; and if they heard, they would not respond to you. On the Day of Resurrection, they will deny your association.[1] And none can inform you like [one] acquainted with all matters. (Soorah Faatir; 35:13-14)

Again, let me turn the question around. What do we mean by *Tawheed al Rububiyyah*?

To believe that Allah alone is the sole, creator and sustainer of all creation.

Good.

---

[1] Of them with Allah or your worship of them.

CHAPTER FOUR

Can I ask about Tawheed Al Asma Wa As Sifaat

What are the *Al Asma Wa As Sifaat*?

These are the Names and Attributes of Allah. Allah has certain names or attributes by which we can call upon him and which we can use to understand him better. He says in the Qur'aan:

$$وَلِلَّهِ ٱلْأَسْمَآءُ ٱلْحُسْنَىٰ فَٱدْعُوهُ بِهَا$$

> And to Allah belong the best names, so invoke Him by them. (Soorah Al A'raaf; 7:180)[1]

What is an attribute?

The word "attribute" means a quality or a feature. For example, you could say that the attribute of a good judge is honesty. Allah has many features and qualities. He has many attributes.

Why are the *Al Asma Wa As Sifaat* so important?

We cannot see Allah. For us Allah is *Bil Ghaib* (in the realms of the Unseen). He is hidden. The only way we can know about Him is to study those words that He has used to describe Himself, those texts from the Qur'aan and a*hadith* (plural of hadith) in which He discusses His Own Names and Attributes.

---

[1] WA- LI- 'ALLAAH AL- ASMAA' AL- H.USNAA FA- UDcO -HU BI- -HAA

So only, by referring to His Names and Attributes, can we really know more about Allah?

Yes. If you do not refer to the *Al Asma Wa As Sifaat*, then you are merely speculating about the Nature of Allah, and therefore entering a very dangerous area indeed.

Is it recommended to learn the *Al Asma Wa As Sifaat* of Allah?

Yes, it is recommended to not only learn His Names and Attributes but also to understand them. Knowledge of His Names and Attributes is the best kind of knowledge a person can acquire. It is one thing to study and excel in the worldly sciences (e.g. Biology, Physics, Economics and so on). But the most excellent subject to acquire knowledge in is knowledge about Allah Himself.

The *aalim* (scholar) Ibn Al Arabi[1], stated that "the excellence and virtue of knowledge is according to the subject matter. The Creator is the Highest and Most Excellent of subject matters and therefore the knowledge of His Names is the Most Excellent and Highest of Knowledge"[2].

What is the evidence encouraging us to learn and understand the Names and Attributes of Allah?

Muhammad sallallahu alayhe wasalam said:

"Allah has ninety-nine Names, one hundred except one, whoever memorises and comprehends them enters paradise." (Narrated by Abu Hurairah in Sahih Bukhari; 9:489)

What does it mean to "memorise and comprehend?"

The word being used here is *Ihsa*. Various *ulema* (scholars) have commented extensively as to what this word means. One of the most notable amongst them, Ibn Al Qayyim, identified three levels to *Al Ihsa*:
1.   Memorisation of the words used and the number;
2.   Understanding their meaning;
3.   Actually supplicating Allah with those Names.

---

[1] Not to be confused with the 12th Century comentator Ibn 'Alee Ibn Arabee of Andalus who held many false and heretical views regarding the attributes of Allah.
[2] Ahkaam Al Qur'aan 2/993.

I suppose doing this is a great exercise in building *eemaan* (faith)?

InshaAllah, when a Muslim strives to increase his knowledge of Islaam and then strives to act upon what he has learnt, his *eemaan* will inevitably be increased. Memorising, understanding and repeating the Names and Attributes of Allah increases *eemaan* and purifies the heart.

Purifies the heart?

When a Muslim truly comes to understand the *Al Asma Wa As Sifaat*, that understanding will be reflected in all aspects of His behaviour. For example:

♦ A Muslim who is battling temptation will find ease when he remembers that Allah is Al A'lam (All Knowing), Al Baseer (All Seeing) and As Samee' (All Hearing);

♦ A Muslim who is sick and in pain will find strength when he remembers that Allah is Ash Shaafee (The One who Cures);

♦ A Muslim who is racked with guilt over the sins he has committed and is truly repentant, will find comfort when he remembers that Allah is Al Ghafour (The Forgiving), Al Ghaffaar (The Oft Forgiving), Al Ghaafir adh Dhanb (The Forgiver of Sin), Ar Rahmaan (The Beneficient), Ar Raheem (The Merciful).

To quote Umar Sulaiman Al Ashqar, "Our knowledge of His (Allah's) Hearing, Sight and Knowledge means that not even the weight of an atom in the heavens nor in the earth is hidden from Him, and that He is aware of secret thoughts, knows the treachery of the eyes and what the hearts conceal. This causes a person to guard his tongue and limbs as well as the whisperings of his heart from everything that does not please Allah.

In addition, he links the limbs to what Allah loves and is pleased with, which in turn creates in him modesty which enables him to avoid what is forbidden and evade shameful deeds.[1]"

How many *Al Asma Wa As Sifaat* does Allah have? Is it ninety-nine as mentioned in the previous hadith?

No. It is "at least" ninety-nine.

Are you sure? I grew up with the figure of ninety-nine. It is a figure firmly planted in my mind as being the number of the Names and Attributes of Allah.

The majority of the *ulema* state that the number mentioned in this *hadith* is not definitive. They state that the Names of Allah, in fact number more than ninety-nine[2].

---

[1] The Names and Attributes of Allah by Sheikh Umar Sulaiman Al Ashqar, English version published by Jam'iat Ihyaa Minhaaj a Sunnah, Suffolk, UK

[2] The number "ninety-nine" is also mentioned in a *hadith* from Tirmidhi, which we will discuss later, InshAllah.

To cite Ibn Hajr Al Asqalani, rahmatullahe alayhe, "Most of the people of knowledge are of the opinion that the most Excellent Names of Allah are not limited to this number (ninety-nine) and that there are more than this."[1]

Some *ulema* assert that the number ninety-nine implies the memorising of any ninety-nine from amongst the greater number of names. Whilst others assert that it refers to ninety-nine specific but hidden Names from that greater total.[2]

So, what is the exact figure?

The commentators of old vary about the number of those Names and Attributes of Allah known to mankind. They vary depending on what system they used to decide whether any particular Name is in fact a Name of Allah.

Why do you say "known to mankind?" Are there names that we don't know about?

Yes. Basically, Allah's *Al Asma Wa As Sifaat* fall into three categories:
1.   Those we know about, to be found in the Qur'aan and *ahadith*;
2.   Those that were revealed to other creations of Allah, but not to us, e.g. those revealed to His angels;
3.   Those Names known by Allah alone and kept hidden from all His creation.

Muhammad sallallahu alayhe wasalam once supplicated to Allah as follows: "I ask you with every one of your Names with which You have named Yourself or You have revealed in Your Book or taught to any one of your creation or which You have kept to Yourself in the Knowledge of the Unseen." (Narrated by Ibn Masud and reported in Ahmed. Authenticated by Ibn Hibban).

One attribute of God I hear often is "omni-presence." Is Allah everywhere?

No. Allah is not "everywhere," as many people mistakenly comment. He is above the Throne. He states in the Qur'aan:

$$\text{إِنَّ رَبَّكُمُ ٱللَّهُ ٱلَّذِى خَلَقَ ٱلسَّمَـٰوَٰتِ وَٱلْأَرْضَ فِى سِتَّةِ أَيَّامٍ}$$

$$\text{ثُمَّ ٱسْتَوَىٰ عَلَى ٱلْعَرْشِ}$$

---

[1] Quoted by Al Ashqar above, pp 61
[2] Discussed by Al Ashqar, pp 64-66

Indeed your Lord is Allah, Who created the heavens and the earth in Six Days, and then established Himself over (*Istawa*) the Throne (really in a manner that suits His Majesty). (Soorah al A'raaf; 7:54)

We know that Allah is above His Glorious Throne. What manner that *"Istawa"* takes we don't know, but it is in a manner that suits His Majesty.

My cousin says that it is "heretical" to deny that Allah is "everywhere?"

We pray that Allah Subhaan Wa T'alaa gives your cousin *hidaayah* and a correct understanding of the *aqeedah* of our pious predecessors. If your cousin asserts, that "Allah is Everywhere," you should politely ask him which *ayaah* of the Qur'aan, *hadith* or commentary of any of the early generation of Muslims, he is quoting from.

The notion that Allah T'aala is everywhere is a false concept that has seaped into Islaam from other philosophies and faiths. Tell me. Do you by any chance know the first line of the Christian supplication, "The Lords Prayer."

Yes. I think it goes, "Our father who art in heaven."

Notice those words "art in." How can Allah be "in" the heaven when he has already informed us that He is "above" the heaven? In fact, how can Allah be "art" in anything! Nothing can contain Allah. Exalted is He above ALL such false notions.

Tell me. What is in your left trouser pocket?

A few coins, my bus pass and a screwed up dirty hanky. I'm sorry, I have a cold!

La Bus, Tahurran InshAllah (You will be purified, InshaAllah). Tell me. Do you think Allah T'aala knows the contents of your left trouser pocket?

Of course He does. He Knows Everything.

Tell me. Do you think He is actually IN your left trouser pocket, WITH your coins, BESIDE your bus pass and NEXT TO your dirty hanky.

No way! Allah is above such a situation.

Yes. Exalted is He above ALL such situations and above such false notions. Allah's knowledge encompasses all things. He knows everything, but we cannot say that He is everywhere[1].

---

[1]Shaykh Abdal Rahmaan Al Barraak comments, "Saying that Allaah is with us, does not mean that He is mixed with (or dwells in) His creation; rather He is with His slaves by His Knowledge. He is above His Throne and nothing is hidden from Him of what they do." Shaykh al Islaam Ibn Taymiyyah stated (in

Tell me about *Tawheed Al Asma Wa As Sifaat*.

Belief in the Unity of the Names and Attributes of Allah is a very important part of *tawheed*. If you deny this part, you deny a major part of *tawheed*.

That is very serious. How can I adhere to *Tawheed Al Asma Wa As Sifaat*?

Here are eleven of the most important things to be careful of[1]:

POINT OF CAUTION NUMBER ONE

It is not permitted to call Allah by a Name which He has not used to describe Himself. Similarly, we cannot call Him by a name which the Messenger sallallahu alayhe was sallam has not told us about as being a Name of Allah.

For example?

We cannot call upon Him with:
- ☒   Al Abad (The Eternal)
- ☒   Al 'Amad (Time)
- ☒   Ath Thabit (The Firm)
- ☒   Al Balee (The Heedful)

What is wrong in calling Him other names if they are good names?

These names may sound nice, but if they were not mentioned by Allah or His messenger sallallahu alayhe wasalam as being amongst His *Asma Wa As Sifaat*, then we cannot use them.

Imagine the following scenario with the Immigration Officer of an international airport:

Sharh al Aqeedat il Wasitiyah) that, "the most perfect among the creatures and the most knowledgeable about their Lord, i.e. Muhammad sallallahu alayhe was sallam, had put a question regarding Allah with the phrase, "Where is He?" He asked a slave girl "Where is Allah?" and he felt pleased with her answer when she said, "In the heaven." Sheikh Munnajid comments on the same hadith above, "This young girl was uneducated, as many are, and she was a slave, but she knew that her Lord is above heaven." He asserts that it is incorrect to say that, "He is neither above or below us, neither to the left nor the right. He is everywhere!" Ad Dhaabi confirms in his His book *Al 'Aluw li'l 'Aliy al Ghaffaar* that *istawa* was the agreed consensus of the *sahabah* and others amongst the *salaf as saleh* (our pious predecessors).

[1] This list comprises eleven items only of the most important things to be careful of with regard to *Al Asma Wa As Sifaat*. This list is not exhaustive and there are other considerations that the *ulema* have noted but which are beyond the scope of this writing.

Officer :	(looking at passport) Name sir?
You :	Bilal Ahmed
Officer :	No. Your name is Khalid.
You :	No it's not. You can see in my passport, it's Bilal.
Officer :	I don't care what it says in the passport. I say your name is Khalid.
You :	But Bilal is what my birth certificate says, Bilal is on all my official papers.
Officer :	Look Mr. Khalid! I don't care what's written anywhere. Your name is Khalid, OK? Now, any more lip from you and it's down to the station, do you understand?
You :	Now just a minute. Bilal is what everybody calls me, Bilal IS my name!
Officer :	OK that's it Mr. Khalid. I've had enough. It's a night in the cells for you!

What a strange, arrogant man?

Yes. If you think that man is strange and arrogant for changing the name of a human, how strange and arrogant are those who call Allah by Names and Attributes that He has not sanctioned for Himself. We call Allah by His Most Beautiful Names and it is absolutely not for us to question why he has chosen those names and not others.

POINT OF CAUTION NUMBER TWO

When calling upon Allah by His Most Beautiful Names, we must not restrict ourselves to those *Al Asma Wa As Sifaat* mentioned in the Qur'aan alone.

There are many names of Allah mentioned in the a*hadith*, but which do not appear in the Qur'aan.

For example?

We can call upon Him with:
- ☑ Al Hannan (The Compassionate)
- ☑ Al Mannan (The Benefactor)
- ☑ As Subuh (The Perfect)
- ☑ As Shaafee (The One Who Cures)
- ☑ Al Muhsin (The Charitable)

POINT OF CAUTION NUMBER THREE

We cannot call upon Allah with made up Names based upon actions of His that we may read about in the Qur'aan.

It is true that He performs those actions or has certain other descriptions. However, if those actions or descriptions were not used by Allah to be considered as one of His Attributes then we cannot accept them as Attributes of Allah.

For example?

1.   Allah says in the Qur'aan (interpretation of the meaning), "Your Lord comes with the angels in rows[1]." However, we cannot call him Al Ja'iee (the One who Comes);
2.   The Qur'aan also mentions (interpretation of the meaning), "And it is He who nourishes me and gives me to drink[2]." However, we cannot refer to Him as Al Mut'im (the Nourisher) or Al Maskee (The One Who gives drink);
3.   The Qur'aan states (interpretation of the meaning), "It was He who supported you with His help[3]." However, we cannot call him Al Mu'ayid (The Supporter).

Neither should we include names that merely give "information" about Allah. Although these names help us know Allah better, they cannot be included as being from His Most Beautiful Names. For example, As Shay (The Thing), Al Mawjood (The Existent)

POINT OF CAUTION NUMBER FOUR

We cannot call upon Allah with Names and Attributes that are blameworthy or reprehensible. Neither can we call Him by Names that He and His messenger sallallahu alayhe wasalam had specifically rejected.

For example?

We cannot call upon Him with:
- ☒   Al Kha'in (The treacherous);
- ☒   Al Faqeer (The poor);
- ☒   Al Ajiz (The unable);
- ☒   Al Maakir (The plotter);
- ☒   Al Faatin (The tempter);
- ☒   As Sakht (The Enraged).

POINT OF CAUTION NUMBER FIVE

Any name that cannot be used for the purposes of Dua (supplication) cannot be included in the Names of Allah[4]. Remember, what Allah states in the Qur'aan:

---

[1] Soorah al Fajr; 89:22
[2] Soorah Ash Shu'ara; 26:79
[3] Soorah Al Anfaal; 8:62
[4] Also, athough they are worthy Names for general supplication, names with the prefix "Dhu" (possesor, owner), cannot be considered as being from amongst the Most Excellent Names of Allah. This opinion is held by the majority of the *ulema*. For example:
- ☒ Dhu Al Quwwah (Possessor of Strength)
- ☒ Dhu Al Kibriya (Possessor of Pride)
- ☒ Dhu Al Rahmah (Possessor of Mercy)

$$\text{وَلِلَّهِ الْأَسْمَاءُ الْحُسْنَىٰ فَادْعُوهُ بِهَا}$$

And to Allah belong the best names, so **invoke Him** by them. (Soorah Al A'raaf; 7:180)[1]

For example?

We cannot call upon Him with:
- ☒ Ad Dahr (Time)
- ☒ Al Abad (The Eternal)
- ☒ Al 'Amad (Time)
- ☒ Al Burhaan (The Proof)
- ☒ Ad Da'ee (The Caller)
- ☒ Ad Daree (The Averter)
- ☒ Az Zari (The One who Causes to Grow)
- ☒ Al Qadi (The Judge)

POINT OF CAUTION NUMBER SIX

Do not attempt to explain or investigate Allah's *Al Asma Wa As Sifaat*. This is called *Taykeef*.

So, what we read is what we accept?

Yes. We must stick firmly to the obvious meanings of His Names and Attributes. We must not speculate or imagine what we feel a particular name or attribute must mean. We must stay with the obvious meaning.

Let me ask you. Allah is described in the Qur'aan as As Samee' (All Hearing).

$$\text{لَيْسَ كَمِثْلِهِ شَيْءٌ وَهُوَ السَّمِيعُ الْبَصِيرُ}$$

There is nothing like unto Him, and He is the Hearing, the Seeing. (Soorah ash Shooraa; 42:11)

☒ Dhu Al Jalaal Wal Ikraam (Possessor of Majesty and Honour)
To cite Al Ashqar (ibid) "Those Names which are mentioned in the Qur'aan and Sunnah which are prefixed by "dhu" and are added to one of Allah's Attributes or Actions or to a part of His creation are one of the greatest ways in which the Lord of Might is praised and supplicated. However, according to most correct opinion, they are not included among His ninety-nine Most Excellent names."

[1] My highlighting – Abu Omar

What is the obvious meaning of *As Samee*?

"He Hears All?"

Yes. We know for sure that Allah "hears" because that's how He has described Himself. However, Allah's hearing is not the same as human hearing because, as He mentions above, "There is nothing whatever like unto Him.." Allah hears, but it is not for us to speculate as to the "nature" of that hearing.

POINT OF CAUTION NUMBER SEVEN

Do not suppose that Allah's Attributes resemble those of His creations.

Can I ask a question?

OK.

Does Allah have hands?

Yes, He does. He mentions this in the Qur'aan:

$$قَالَ يَـٰٓإِبۡلِيسُ مَا مَنَعَكَ أَن تَسۡجُدَ لِمَا خَلَقۡتُ بِيَدَىَّ أَسۡتَكۡبَرۡتَ أَمۡ كُنتَ$$

$$مِنَ ٱلۡعَالِينَ ۝$$

(Allah) said: "O Iblees (Satan)! What prevented you from prostrating to that which I created with My Hands? Were you arrogant [then], or were you [already] among the haughty? (Soorah Saad; 38:75)

Does Allah have eyes?

Yes.

$$وَٱصۡبِرۡ لِحُكۡمِ رَبِّكَ فَإِنَّكَ بِأَعۡيُنِنَا وَسَبِّحۡ بِحَمۡدِ رَبِّكَ حِينَ تَقُومُ ۝$$

And be patient [O Muhammad], for the Decision of your Lord, for indeed, you are in Our Eyes [i.e. sight]. And exalt [Allah] with praise of your Lord when you arise. (Soorah Tur; 52:48)

Does Allah have a face or a foot?

Yes. These are mentioned in the Qur'aan and a*hadith*.

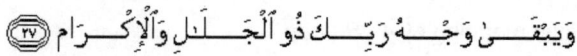

And there will remain the Face of your Lord, Owner of Majesty and Honour. (Soorah Ar Rahmaan; 55:27)

Anas radhiAllaho anho narrates that the Prophet sallallahu said, "The people will be thrown into the (Hell) Fire and it will say: "Are there any more (to come)?' (50.30) till Allah puts His Foot over it and it will say, 'Qati! Qati! (Enough! Enough!)' " (Sahih Al Bukhari 6:371)

If we say He has all these things, aren't we guilty of comparing His Attributes to those of His creation?

No. Remember, we accept that Allah has all the Attributes (Hearing, sight, foot, face, hands) which you have mentioned,[1] BUT we do so:
1.   without knowing what form those Attributes take
AND
2.   understanding that, whatever the nature of those attributes, they are not the same as human attributes.

Many religions make statues of their gods. Is this an example of breach of *Tawheed Al Asma Wa As Sifaat*?

Yes. This is *shirk*. Hindus and Buddhists, for example, manufacture idols to give a physical representation to god, as they perceive him to be. This is unacceptable in Islaam with respect to Allah.

Even Christians, who are themselves *Ehle Kitaab* (People of the Book), represent god in their icons and paintings. Either they draw or paint him directly (a la Michael Angelo) or they do carvings and pictures of Christ himself, whom they claim to be god.

When they mould these models and draw these pictures, how do they know what god looks like?

Yes. How do they know? They don't know and neither do Muslims. We cannot speculate about any Attribute of Allah and we certainly cannot suppose that those Attributes are like human attributes. The Qur'aan makes it clear (interpretation of the meaning), "Nor is there to Him any equivalent" (Soorah al Ikhlaas; 112:4)

---

[1] In fact, we must accept them because we have been told about them.

The Christians say that Allah made this world in six days and on seventh day he rested. I would imagine that this is completely contrary to the concept of *Tawheed Al Asma Wa As Sifaat*?

Yes, it is. Sleep, hunger, fatigue, envy, jealousy and so on are all frailties and failings felt by humans. They are features of Allah's creation, NOT of Allah Himself.

POINT OF CAUTION NUMBER EIGHT

Do not give man or any of Allah's creations, the Attributes of Allah.

It is not permissible to say of any human that for example,
- ☒   He has control over destiny or
- ☒   He is the creator of everything in the universe or
- ☒   He has god like powers or
- ☒   He is the Most Merciful or
- ☒   He has knowledge of *Al Ghaib* (Unseen) or
- ☒   He can change past and future events etc.

These are examples of Allah's Sublime Attributes and under no circumstances can they be applied to humans or any of Allah's creation.

POINT OF CAUTION NUMBER NINE

Do not give idols the attributes of Allah.

This was done by the Quraish at the time of Muhammad sallallahu alayhe wasalam. For example, they named one of their idols Al-Lat, a name derived from Allah.

POINT OF CAUTION NUMBER TEN

Do not deny any or all of the valid Names and Attributes of Allah. This is called *Ta'teel*.

Again, the Quraish were amongst those guilty of this. They refused to acknowledge the Most Beautiful Names of Allah being presented to them. This stubbornness is mentioned in the Qur'aan, (interpretation of the meaning), "while they disbelieve in the Most Merciful." (Soorah ar Ra'd; 13:30)

POINT OF CAUTION NUMBER ELEVEN

Be careful with the use of the Word "Abd" when connecting it to the attributes of Allah.

The word "Abd" in Arabic means "slave." Where a person is named with one of the Al Asma Wa As Sifaat, this word must be placed before his name. So for example, we are not permitted to call anybody simply "Ar Rehmaan" (The Beneficient). He must be called Abdar Rehmaan" (Slave of the Beneficient)[1].

Tell me would you call somebody "Allah?"

No! never!

Of course, you wouldn't. That would be strange, outrageous and a big sin. However, you can call someone AbdAllah (Slave of Allah).

I have a friend called *Abd Ar Rasool*. Is this acceptable?

No. Your friends Name means "Slave of the Messenger." This is totally unacceptable. The word "Abd" can only be used alongside the Names and Attributes of Allah. You cannot use it before names or titles of people. So, you could not say, for example, Abd Al Muhammad, Abd Al Hussain, Abd Al Ali, Abd An *Nabi* and so on.

Alhamdulilah, I will, InshaAllah, try my very best to adhere to *Tawheed al Al Asma Wa As Sifaat.*

If you do that you will be rewarded, InshAllah. Avoiding *shirk* and safeguarding *tawheed* is amongst the noblest acts of a Muslim.

I will, InshaAllah, memorise, understand and actually start reciting the Names of Allah. My uncle has a list of ninety-nine names on his wall. I will refer to that.

Well, actually, you have to be careful. The picture you refer to is most probably based upon a *hadith* recorded by the eminent collector of a*hadith*, Tirmidhi. Whilst most of the names detailed in the Tirmidhi list are acceptable, the list does present a number of problems.

1. It is agreed by the scholars of a*hadith* to be weak. It has been critisised both for its poor chain of narrators and contradictions in content.
2. It mentions names that are not acceptable according to some of the rules already mentioned e.g. Dhu Al Jallaale Wal Ikraam, As Saalim.
3. It does not mention some names that are referred to in the Qur'aan and Sunnah and are accepted as being amongst Allah's Names.
4. By mentioning "ninety-nine" names exactly, it assumes a restriction on the number of Allah's Names. As we have already discussed, the *ulema* are in

---

[1] The Canadian *aalim*, Abu Ameenah Bilal Phillips comments that for certain of the Divine Names, where they are mentioned in their indefinite form (i.e. without "Al" before them), then "Abd" is not necessary. So someone can be called Raheem (Merciful) so long as he is not called Ar Raheem (The Merciful), in which case "Abd" would be required.

agreement that the number is more than ninety-nine. The renowned scholar Ibn Taymiyyah has commented that "No authentic *hadith* has been reported from the Prophet sallallahu alayhe wasalam that specifies the ninety-nine names of Allah[1]."

OK. So if I can't rely on this famous hadith, what can I safely consider to be the Names of Allah?

Below is a full list of over one hundred Names and Attributes mentioned in the Qur'aan and *ahadith*.

I hope this chapter has shown you how important the remembrance of Allah's *Al Asma Wa As Sifaat* are and how careful we must be with regard to them.

Keep them in your heart always, adopt the points of caution mentioned here and do not sit in the company of those who simply don't care.

وَلِلَّهِ ٱلْأَسْمَآءُ ٱلْحُسْنَىٰ فَٱدْعُوهُ بِهَا ۖ وَذَرُواْ ٱلَّذِينَ يُلْحِدُونَ فِىٓ أَسْمَٰٓئِهِۦ ۚ

سَيُجْزَوْنَ مَا كَانُواْ يَعْمَلُونَ ﴿١٨٠﴾

And to Allah belong the best names, so invoke Him by them. And leave [the company of] those who practice deviation[2] concerning His names. They will be recompensed for what they have been doing. (Soorah Al A'raaf; 7:180)

---

[1] Majmu' al Fataawaa – Sheikh al Islaam; 22/482
[2] i.e. use them improperly or deny them.

Some of the Names and Attributes of Allah mentioned in the Qur'aan and ahadith.[1]

1. Allah
2. Al Ilah, The God [43:84]
3. Al Awwal, The First [57:3]
4. Al Aakhir, The Last [57:3]
5. Al Akram, The Most Bountiful [96:3]
6. Al A'ala, The Most High [86:1]
7. Al Ahad, The One [112:1]
8. Al Badee', The Originator [2-117]
9. Al Baaree, The Originator [59:24]
10. Al Barr, The Benign [52:28]
11. Al Baatin, The Immanent [57:3]
12. Al Baasit, The Munificent [Ibn Majah]
13. Al Baseer, The All Seeing [22:61]
14. At Tawwaab, The Relenting [2:160]
15. Aj Jabbaar, The Compeller [59:23]
16. Aj Jaami', The Gatherer [4:140]
17. Aj Jawaad, The Magnanimous [ath Tirmidhi]
18. Aj Jameel, The Beautiful [Muslim]
19. Al Haleem, The Forbearing [22:59]
20. Al Hakeem, The Wise [59:24]
21. Al Hayy, The Living [2:255]
22. Al Haseeb, The Reckoner [4:6]
23. Al Hafeedh, The Preserver [11:57]
24. Al Hameed, The Praiseworthy [22:64]
25. Al Haqq, The Truth [22:62]
26. Al Hakam, The Arbiter [6:114]
27. Al Hafee, Al Gracious [19:47]

28. Al Hannaan, The Compassionate [Ahmed]
29. Al Hayyee, The Modest [Ahmad, Abu Dawood, An Nasaa'ee]
30. Al Khaaliq, The Creator [59:24]
31. Al Khallaaq, The Creator [15:86]
32. Al Khabeer, The All Aware [22:63]
33. Ad Dayaan, The One Who Judges after Reckoning [Bukhari]
34. Ar Rahmaan, The Beneficent [55:1]
35. Ar Raheem, The Merciful [59:23]
36. Ar Razzaaq, The Provider [51:58]
37. Ar Raqeeb, The Watchful [4:1]
38. Ar Ra'ouf, The Most Kind [22:65]
39. Ar Rabb, The Lord [1:2]
40. Ar Rafeeq, The Gentle [Ibn Majah]
41. As Sateer, The One Who Veils [Ahmed, Abu Dawood, An Nasaa'ee]
42. As Sayyad, The Master [Ahmad]
43. As Samee', The All Hearing [22:61]
44. As Subouh, The Perfect [Muslim]
45. Ash Shukour, The Appreciative [42:23]
46. Ash Shaakir, The Rewarding [2:158]
47. Ash Shaafee, The One Who Cures [Bukhari]
48. As Samad, The Eternally Besought of by All [112:2]
49. As Saadiq, The Truthful [6:146]
50. At Tayyib, The Good [Ath Tirmidhi]
51. Adh Dhaahir, The Evident [57:3]
52. Al 'Azeez, The Mighty [59:23]
53. Al 'Aalim, The Knower [30:50]
54. Al Aleem, The Aware [22:59]
55. Al 'Allaam, The All Knower [9:94]
56. Al 'Alee, The High [2:255]
57. Al Azeem, The Immense [2:255]
58. Al 'Afou, The Pardoner [22:60]
59. Al Ghafour, The Forgiving [22:60]
60. Al Ghaffaar, The Oft-Forgiving [39:5]
61. Al Ghaafir, The Forgiver of Sin [40:3]
62. Al Ghanee, The Self Sufficient [22:64]
63. Al Faatir, The Originator [35:1]
64. Al Fattaah, The Judge [34:26]
65. Al Qahhaar, The Irresistible [39:4]
66. Al Quddous, The Holy [59:23]

---

[1] The research for this table is primarily based upon the work of a leading aalim in this area, Sheikh 'Umar Sulaiman Al-Ashqar and his book, "The Names and Attributes of Allah, According to the Doctrine of Ahlus Sunnah wal Jama'ah". I have tried to be as thorough and meticulous as possible in my own research of the research of the scholars. I seek Allah's pleasure only and not His wrath. If you notice anything detailed here contrary to the Qur'an and sunnah, please advise me as soon as possible. I ask Allah's forgiveness for anything misleading or incorrect. Abu Omar. (Numbers in brackets related to Qur'aanic Soorah and Ayaah. Other references are collections of *ahadith*)

67. Al Qareeb, The Near [11:61]
68. Al Qayyoum, The Sustainer [2:255]
69. Al Qaadir, The Able [6:65]
70. Al Qadeer, The Potent [60:7]
71. Al Qawwee, The All Powerful [8:52]
72. Al Qaabid, The Constrictor [Ibn Majah]
73. Al Kabeer, The Great [22:62]
74. Al Kareem, The Most Generous [82:6]
75. Al Kafeel, The Guarantor [16:91]
76. Al Lateef, The Subtle [22:63]
77. Al Maalik, The Owner [1:3]
78. Al Malik, The Sovereign Lord [59:23]
79. Al Maleek, The King [54:55]
80. Al Mu'min, The Guardian [59:23]
81. Al Mujeeb, The Responsive [11:61]
82. Al Muhaymin, The Guardian [59:23]
83. Al Mutakabbir, The Proud [59:23]
84. Al Mussawwir, The Fashioner [59:24]
85. Al Mateen, The Firm [51:58]
86. Al Muqeet, The Overseer [4:85]
87. Al Majeed, The Glorious [11:73]
88. Al Muqtadir, The Omnipotent [54:55]

89. Al Musta'aan, The One Whose Help is Sought [21:112]
90. Al Muhyeey, The Giver of Life [41:39]
91. Al Muta'aalee, The Most High [13:9]
92. Al Mannaan, The Benefactor [Ahmed, Abu Dawood, An Nasaa'ee]
93. Al Muhsin, The Charitable [al Kaamil]
94. Al Maajid, The Illustrious [Ath Tirmidhi]
95. Al Muqaddim, The Advancer [Bukhari]
96. Al Mu'akhkhir, The Retarder [Bukhari]
97. Al Mus'irr, The Price Setter [Ibn Majah]
98. An Naseer, The Helper [4:45]
99. An Nadheef, The Pure [ath Tirmidhi]
100. An Nour, The Light [24:35]
101. Al Haadee, The Guide [25:31]
102. Al Wahhaab, The Bestower [3:8]
103. Al Wassi', The Vast [2:268]
104. Al Wadoud, The Loving [85:14]
105. Al Waarith, The Inheritor [15:23]
106. Al Waleey, The Protector [42:28]
107. Al Waahid, The One [39:4]
108. Al Witr, The Single [Muslim]

CHAPTER FIVE

Can I ask about Al Malaika [The Angels]?

Al Malaika are the servants of Allah. They obey his commands and constantly worship Him. In English, *malaika* are commonly known as "angels."

Are *malaika* the same as us, human beings?

No. *malaika* are a separate creation altogether. Humans were made by Allah from sounding clay. *Jinns*, another creation, were made from smokeless fire. *malaika* however, were made from *noor* (light)[1].

OK, so we may be made differently, but just like *malaika*, we also worship and obey Allah. In that way, aren't we the same?

Many of us humans do worship and obey Allah. But then again, many of us don't. Furthermore, those of us who do obey Allah, are often not obedient all of the time. Even good Muslims sometimes lapse into minor sin (May Allah preserve us from any sin).

This is not the case with *malaika*. EVERY SINGLE *malaika* is ALWAYS obedient to Allah. They worship Allah constantly, without ever faltering. They never incur His anger or displeasure. They never commit sin.

They never commit sin? How is this possible?

That's the way they were created by Allah. Unlike humans and *jinn*, they do not possess free will.

---

[1] Sahih Muslim

Free Will?

Yes, free will, the ability to choose whether to do good or bad. We, as humans, can choose either to follow siraat al mustaqeem (the straight path) or to follow the path of wrongdoing and sin.

So, malaika do not have such a choice?

No, they don't. They were created without the free will to choose between doing good and doing evil. They only do good.

Consequently, there is no such thing as a bad angel, a sinful angel or as is sometimes said in the non-Muslim world, a "fallen" angel. Allah states:

وَمَا نَتَنَزَّلُ إِلَّا بِأَمْرِ رَبِّكَ لَهُۥ مَا بَيْنَ أَيْدِينَا وَمَا خَلْفَنَا وَمَا بَيْنَ

ذَٰلِكَ وَمَا كَانَ رَبُّكَ نَسِيًّا ﴿٦٤﴾

[Jibra'eel said[1]] "And we [angels] descend not except by the order of your Lord. To Him belongs that before us and that behind us and what is in between. And never is your Lord forgetful. (Soorah Maryam 19:64)

You say that malaika never do bad. I thought that Iblees (Shaytaan[2]) was one of the malaika. Was he not a malaika, who disobeyed Allah and became rejected?

The incident you refer to is mentioned a number of times in the Qur'aan. Allah created Aadam alayhe salaam (Adam) and then asked the malaika and jinn to do sajda (prostration) before His new creation. Iblees refused. The Qur'aan mentions:

قَالَ مَا مَنَعَكَ أَلَّا تَسْجُدَ إِذْ أَمَرْتُكَ قَالَ أَنَا خَيْرٌ مِّنْهُ خَلَقْتَنِى مِن

نَّارٍ وَخَلَقْتَهُۥ مِن طِينٍ ﴿١٢﴾

[Allah] said: "What prevented you from prostrating when I commanded you?" [Satan] said: "I am better than he: You created me from fire and created him from clay [i.e. earth]." (Soorah al A'raaf; 7:12)

Notice what Iblees says here, "You created me from fire and created him from clay."

---

[1] in answer to the Prophet's [sallallahu alayhe was sallam] wish that Jibra'eel (Gabriel) would visit him more often.
[2] Satan

43

Fire. This means he is a *jinn*?

Yes. Iblees was a *jinn*. Contrary to popular belief, he was NOT a *malaika*. Just like you and I, he had the choice to obey or disobey Allah. Unfortunately for him, he chose the path of disobedience.

Don't angels become weary or tired from their worship of Allah?

No. The Qur'aan mentions:

يُسَبِّحُونَ ٱلَّيْلَ وَٱلنَّهَارَ لَا يَفْتُرُونَ ۝

> They celebrate His praises by night and by day. And they never flag (nor feel themselves above it).[1]

There are countless angels constantly doing *dhikr* (remembrance of Allah), and others in continuous *ruku* (bowing) and *sujood* (prostration) before Him.

Allah, Himself, must love them dearly?

Yes. Anyone who is an enemy to the *malaika*, is an enemy to Allah.

مَن كَانَ عَدُوًّا لِّلَّهِ وَمَلَـٰٓئِكَتِهِۦ وَرُسُلِهِۦ وَجِبْرِيلَ وَمِيكَـٰلَ

فَإِنَّ ٱللَّهَ عَدُوٌّ لِّلْكَـٰفِرِينَ ۝

> Whoever is an enemy to Allah and His angels and His messengers and Jibreel and Mikaeel – then indeed Allah is an enemy to the disbelievers. (Soorah al Baqarah; 2:98)

You mentioned Jibra'eel and Mikaeel. Who are they?

A number of *malaika* are actually mentioned in the Qur'aan or *ahadith* either by name or title. They are as follows:

- ***Jibreel*** - He is the most important of all the *malaika*. He was the *malaika* through whom the Qur'aan was revealed to Muhammad sallallahu alayhe wasalam.
- ***Mika'eel*** - Once again one of the *malaika* closest to Allah and mentioned in the Qur'aan.
- ***Israfeel*** – He is deputed to sound the deafening and terrifying trumpet at the initiation of *Yawm al Qiyamah* (Day of Resurrection) He is mentioned by Name in a*hadith*[1].

---

[1] i.e. multitudes of angels who never become tired or arrogant.

- **Malik Al Mawt** (The Angel of Death) – He leads those angels responsible for carrying our souls away at death, either violently or in comfort.
- **Munkar and Nakeer** – The angels who ask the initial questions of us in our graves.
- **Maalik** – The Chief Guard of Hellfire
- **Haruth and Maruth** – Two angels mentioned in Soorah al Baqarah. They were sent as a test to the people of Babylon.
- **Kiraaman Khatibeen** – The Noble Recorders recording our deeds.

I have a non-Muslim friend who tells me that angels are the stuff of children's stories. He says they don't really exist. As Muslims, are we required to believe totally in the *malaika*?

Yes. Absolutely, without question. Belief in the *malaika* is one of the *arkaan al eemaan*, pillars of faith. You cannot claim to believe in the other parts of faith, but then decide not to believe in *malaika*.

Malaika are part of *Al ghaib* (the unseen). Even though we cannot see *malaika*, we must believe they exist. If we do not, we fall outside Islaam and into the same state of *kufr* (disbelief) as your non-Muslim friend. Allah makes this very clear in the Qur'aan:

$$ يَـٰٓأَيُّهَا ٱلَّذِينَ ءَامَنُوٓاْ ءَامِنُواْ بِٱللَّهِ وَرَسُولِهِۦ وَٱلۡكِتَـٰبِ ٱلَّذِى نَزَّلَ عَلَىٰ رَسُولِهِۦ وَٱلۡكِتَـٰبِ ٱلَّذِىٓ أَنزَلَ مِن قَبۡلُ وَمَن يَكۡفُرۡ بِٱللَّهِ وَمَلَـٰٓئِكَتِهِۦ وَكُتُبِهِۦ وَرُسُلِهِۦ وَٱلۡيَوۡمِ ٱلۡأَخِرِ فَقَدۡ ضَلَّ ضَلَـٰلَۢا بَعِيدًا ۝ $$

O you who have believed, believe in Allah and his Messenger and the Book that He has sent down upon His Messenger and the Scripture which He sent down before. And who disbelieves in Allah, His angels, His Books, His messengers and the Last Day has certainly gone, far astray. (Soorah an Nisaa'; 4:136)

Are *malaika* always in *Al Ghaib* (the Unseen)?

Generally speaking, yes. They remain invisible to us. However, if Allah Wills, they can become visible[2]. During the time of the *anbiya* (prophets), *malaika* had been known to

---

[1] Tirmidhi

[2] In fact, one animal that is noted as being able to see malaika are cockrels. Abu Hurairah narrates that Allah's Apostle sallAllahu alayhe wasalam said, "When you hear the crowing of cocks, ask for Allah's Blessings for (their crowing indicates that) they have seen an angel. And when you hear the braying of donkeys, seek refuge with Allah from Satan for (their braying indicates) that they have seen a Satan." (Sahih Bukhari; 4:522)

come down in the form of humans. They relayed messages to the Prophets of Allah and helped them in their struggles.

Can you give me some examples?

Ibraheem alayhe salaam (Abraham)

malaika approached him to let him know that, despite his old age, his wife was to have a son, (Ishaaq alayhe salaam – [Isaac]):

هَلْ أَتَـٰكَ حَدِيثُ ضَيْفِ إِبْرَٰهِيمَ ٱلْمُكْرَمِينَ ۝ إِذْ دَخَلُوا۟ عَلَيْهِ فَقَالُوا۟ سَلَـٰمًا قَالَ سَلَـٰمٌ قَوْمٌ مُّنكَرُونَ ۝ فَرَاغَ إِلَىٰٓ أَهْلِهِۦ فَجَآءَ بِعِجْلٍ سَمِينٍ ۝ فَقَرَّبَهُۥٓ إِلَيْهِمْ قَالَ أَلَا تَأْكُلُونَ ۝ فَأَوْجَسَ مِنْهُمْ خِيفَةً قَالُوا۟ لَا تَخَفْ وَبَشَّرُوهُ بِغُلَـٰمٍ عَلِيمٍ ۝ فَأَقْبَلَتِ ٱمْرَأَتُهُۥ فِى صَرَّةٍ فَصَكَّتْ وَجْهَهَا وَقَالَتْ عَجُوزٌ عَقِيمٌ ۝ قَالُوا۟ كَذَٰلِكِ قَالَ رَبُّكِ إِنَّهُۥ هُوَ ٱلْحَكِيمُ ٱلْعَلِيمُ ۝

Has there reached you the story of the honored guests of Abraham?[1] When they entered upon him and said, "[We greet you with] peace" He answered "[And upon you] peace;" [you are] a people unknown." Then he went to his family and came with a fat [roasted] calf, and placed it near them.

He said "Will you not eat?" And he felt from them apprehension. They said ""Fear not" and gave him good tidings of a learned boy. And his wife approached with a cry [of alarm] and struck her face and said: "[I am] a barren old woman!"

They said "Thus has said your Lord: indeed, He is the Wise, the Knowing. (Soorah adh Dhaariyaat; 51:24-30)

Zakariya alayhe salaam (Zacharias)

malaika came to inform him of the immenent birth of Yahya alayhe salaam:

---

[1] Who were angels given honoured positions by Allah.

46

$$هُنَالِكَ دَعَا زَكَرِيَّا رَبَّهُ قَالَ رَبِّ هَبْ لِى مِن لَّدُنكَ ذُرِّيَّةً طَيِّبَةً$$

$$إِنَّكَ سَمِيعُ ٱلدُّعَآءِ ۝ فَنَادَتْهُ ٱلْمَلَٰٓئِكَةُ وَهُوَ قَآئِمٌ يُصَلِّى فِى$$

$$ٱلْمِحْرَابِ أَنَّ ٱللَّهَ يُبَشِّرُكَ بِيَحْيَىٰ مُصَدِّقًا بِكَلِمَةٍ مِّنَ ٱللَّهِ وَسَيِّدًا$$

$$وَحَصُورًا وَنَبِيًّا مِّنَ ٱلصَّٰلِحِينَ ۝ قَالَ رَبِّ أَنَّىٰ يَكُونُ لِى غُلَٰمٌ$$

$$وَقَدْ بَلَغَنِىَ ٱلْكِبَرُ وَٱمْرَأَتِى عَاقِرٌ قَالَ كَذَٰلِكَ ٱللَّهُ يَفْعَلُ مَا يَشَآءُ$$

۝

At that Zacharias called upon His Lord, saying, My Lord! grant me from yourself a good offspring, Indeed you are the Hearer of supplication."

So the angels called him while he was standing in prayer in the chamber, "Indeed Allah gives you good tidings of Yahya, confirming a Word from Allah and [who will be] honourable abstaining [from women], and a prophet from among the righteous."

He said: "My Lord, how will I have a boy when I have reached old age and my wife is barren?" He [the angel] said, "Such is Allah; He does what He wills." (Soorah Aali 'Imraan; 3:38-40)

Maryam alayhe salaam (Mary), The mother of Esa alayhe salaam (Jesus)

The angel Jibra'eel alayhe salaam came to Maryam in the form of a man. He came to announce to her the birth of Esa alayhe salaam. At first she was scared. She did not know who Jibra'eel was and asked him to leave her be. However, he assured her as follows:

$$فَٱتَّخَذَتْ مِن دُونِهِمْ حِجَابًا فَأَرْسَلْنَآ إِلَيْهَا رُوحَنَا فَتَمَثَّلَ$$

$$لَهَا بَشَرًا سَوِيًّا ۝ قَالَتْ إِنِّىٓ أَعُوذُ بِٱلرَّحْمَٰنِ مِنكَ إِن كُنتَ$$

$$تَقِيًّا ۝ قَالَ إِنَّمَآ أَنَا۠ رَسُولُ رَبِّكِ لِأَهَبَ لَكِ غُلَٰمًا زَكِيًّا ۝$$

And she took in seclusion from them, a screen. Then We sent to her Our angel and he represented himself to her as a well proportioned man. She said:

47

"Indeed I seek refuge in The Most Merciful from you, [so leave me], if you should be fearing of Allah." He said: "I am only the messenger of your Lord to give you [news of] a pure boy [i.e. a son]. (Soorah Maryam; 19:17-19)

malaika also came to Loot alayhe salaam to warn him that his city was to be destroyed by Allah. They instructed him to leave the city immediately.

Did the *malaika* make themselves known to Muhammad sallallahu alayhe wasalam?

Yes. It was Jibra'eel who recited the first words of the Qur'aan to Muhammad sallallahu alayhe wasalam in Hira Cave on *Jabbal Noor* (Mount Noor).

Muhammad sallallahu alayhe wasalam continued to receive the Qur'aan through Jibra'eel.

Did the *malaika* help Muhammad sallallahu alayhe wasalam and the new community of Muslims?

Yes. By Allah's command, they constantly aided Muhammad sallallahu alayhe wasalam and his followers.

$$إِن تَتُوبَآ إِلَى ٱللَّهِ فَقَدْ صَغَتْ قُلُوبُكُمَا ۖ وَإِن تَظَٰهَرَا عَلَيْهِ فَإِنَّ ٱللَّهَ هُوَ$$

$$مَوْلَىٰهُ وَجِبْرِيلُ وَصَٰلِحُ ٱلْمُؤْمِنِينَ ۖ وَٱلْمَلَٰٓئِكَةُ بَعْدَ ذَٰلِكَ ظَهِيرٌ ﴿٤﴾$$

If you two[1] repent to Allah [it is best], for your hearts have deviated. But if cooperate against him[2] then indeed Allah is his Protector and Jibreel the righteous of the believers and the angels, moreover, are [his] assistants. (Soorah at Tahreem; 66:4)

At the Battle of Badr, the Muslim army was outnumbered by the *kuffaar*, three to one. However, Allah fortified their ranks with an army of one thousand *malaika*.

$$إِذْ تَسْتَغِيثُونَ رَبَّكُمْ فَٱسْتَجَابَ لَكُمْ أَنِّى مُمِدُّكُم بِأَلْفٍ مِّنَ ٱلْمَلَٰٓئِكَةِ$$

$$مُرْدِفِينَ ﴿٩﴾$$

---

[1] The "two" in question here are the wives of Muhammad sallAllahu alayhe wasalam, Aisha and Hafsa radhiAllaho anhumma.

[2] Muhammad sallAllahu alayhe wasalam

[Remember] when you asked help of your Lord and He answered you, "Indeed I will reinforce you with a thousand from the angels, following one another. (Soorah al Anfaal; 8:9)

Did those *malaika* actually fight?

Yes. They did. Both the Muslims and the *kuffaar* witnessed the *malaika* fighting in the thick of battle. These reports are clearly documented in the sahih a*hadith*.

The *malaika*, led by Jibreel alay salam himself, were brave and ruthless warriors. They were seen striking off the heads of *kuffaar* with their swords, rescuing Muslims from immeanent danger and capturing *kuffaar* prisoners of war.

So, it seems Muhammad sallallahu alayhe wasalam always had the angels on his side?

Yes. Furthermore, they were always wishing blessings upon him:

$$\text{إِنَّ ٱللَّهَ وَمَلَـٰٓئِكَتَهُۥ يُصَلُّونَ عَلَى ٱلنَّبِىِّ يَـٰٓأَيُّهَا ٱلَّذِينَ ءَامَنُواْ صَلُّواْ عَلَيْهِ}$$

$$\text{وَسَلِّمُواْ تَسْلِيمًا ۝}$$

Indeed Allah confers blessing upon the Prophet, and His angels [ask Him to do so]. O you who have believed, ask [Allah to confer] blessing upon him and ask [Allah to grant him] peace. (Soorah al Ahzaab; 33:56)

How many *malaika* are there?

There are more than we could ever imagine. The actual figure? *Allah hu 'alim* (Allah Knows Best). Allahs says (interpretation of the meaning), "And how many angels there are in the heavens," (Soorah an Najm; 53:26).

At the very least, there are twice the number of *malaika* that there are human beings on earth, because each and every one of us has two *malaika* watching over us recording all our deeds.

ALL our deeds?

Yes. At Allah's command, they are with us constantly, noting down ALL our good or bad deeds. Every single action, however big or small is being written down. Nothing escapes being recorded. Allah reminds us of this:

$$ سَوَآءٌ مِّنكُم مَّنْ أَسَرَّ ٱلْقَوْلَ وَمَن جَهَرَ بِهِۦ $$

$$ وَمَنْ هُوَ مُسْتَخْفٍ بِٱلَّيْلِ وَسَارِبٌۢ بِٱلنَّهَارِ ۝ لَهُۥ مُعَقِّبَٰتٌ $$

$$ مِّنۢ بَيْنِ يَدَيْهِ وَمِنْ خَلْفِهِۦ يَحْفَظُونَهُۥ مِنْ أَمْرِ ٱللَّهِ $$

It is the same [to Him] concerning you whether one conceals [his] speech or one publicises it and whether one is hidden by night or conspicuous [among others] by day. For him [i.e. each one] are successive [angels[1]] before and behind him, who protect Him by the Decree of Allah[2]. (Soorah ar Ra'd; 13:10-11)

Do these angels have names?

They are called *Kiraaman Khaatibeen* (Noble Recorders). They sit on either side of us:

$$ إِذْ يَتَلَقَّى ٱلْمُتَلَقِّيَانِ عَنِ ٱلْيَمِينِ وَعَنِ ٱلشِّمَالِ قَعِيدٌ ۝ مَّا يَلْفِظُ $$

$$ مِن قَوْلٍ إِلَّا لَدَيْهِ رَقِيبٌ عَتِيدٌ ۝ $$

When the two receivers [i.e. recording angels] receive, seated on the right and on the left. He [i.e. man] does not utter any word except that with Him is an observer prepared [to record]. (Soorah Qaaf; 50:17-18)

Do the *malaika* have wings?

Yes, they do. We know this because we are told so in the Qur'aan and a*hadith*.

$$ ٱلْحَمْدُ لِلَّهِ فَاطِرِ ٱلسَّمَٰوَٰتِ وَٱلْأَرْضِ جَاعِلِ ٱلْمَلَٰئِكَةِ رُسُلًا أُو۟لِىٓ أَجْنِحَةٍ $$

$$ مَّثْنَىٰ وَثُلَٰثَ وَرُبَٰعَ يَزِيدُ فِى ٱلْخَلْقِ مَا يَشَآءُ إِنَّ ٱللَّهَ عَلَىٰ كُلِّ شَىْءٍ $$

$$ قَدِيرٌ ۝ $$

[All] Praise is due to Allah, Creator of the heavens and the earth [who] made the angels messengers having wings two or three or four. He increases in

---

[1] replacing each other by turn.

[2] The phrase may also be rendered, "…who guard him from [everything except] the Decree of Allah."

Creation what He wills. Indeed, Allah is over all things competent. (Soorah Faatir; 35:1)

Also in Sahih Bukhari (2/336), narrated by Jabir bin Abdullah mentions the presence of *malaika* at the time his father was made *shaheed (*martyred*)*

> "When my father was martyred, I lifted the sheet from his face and wept and the people forbade me to do so but the Prophet did not forbid me. Then my aunt Fatima began weeping and the Prophet said, "It is all the same whether you weep or not. The angels were shading him continuously with their wings till you shifted him (from the field)."

Having said that, it is not for us to speculate at all as to what those wings look like, or indeed what *malaika* themselves look like.

So, we cannot imagine for ourselves what they look like, or draw pictures of them?

No. Speculating about what *al malaika* look like or representing that speculation in the form of a painting or sculpture, is a major sin in Islaam. In the non-Muslim world, you will find many depictions of angels, for example:

☒ As small naked babies (cherubs);
☒ As cupids with bows and arrows;
☒ As partially naked women;
☒ As human beings with wings and haloes (shining circles) above their heads.

This is all speculation based upon nothing more than conjecture. We must just accept them as devoted servants of Allah and not waste our time contemplating what they really may or may not look like. If we do wish to contemplate their appearance, then we must limit ourselves strictly to what we are told about them in the Qur'aan and *ahadith*.

Are the *malaika* male or female?

Allah Knows Best what the angels are. The *kuffaar* in Makkah used to claim that they were female, without any knowledge at all. Such comments bought down severe words from Allah:

أَفَأَصْفَىٰكُمْ رَبُّكُم بِٱلْبَنِينَ وَٱتَّخَذَ مِنَ ٱلْمَلَـٰٓئِكَةِ إِنَـٰثًا إِنَّكُمْ لَتَقُولُونَ قَوْلًا عَظِيمًا ﴿﷽﴾

Then has your Lord (O Pagans!) chosen you for [having] sons and taken [i.e. adopted] from among the angels daughters? Indeed you say a grave saying. (Soorah al Israa'; 17:40)

Daughters? This is *shirk*, is it not?

Yes. It is a gross *shirk* to claim that *malaika* are daughters of Allah. This is a complete breach of *Tawheed al Uluhiyya* (Unity in Worship) and a sin which, if not repented for, will remain unforgivable. Remember. Allah has no sons, daughters, mother, father etc. Nothing is equal to Him. He gave birth to nothing. He created everything and that includes the *malaika*.

Will we see angels after we die?

Yes. The angels will be our first visitors when we are finally alone in our graves. They will initiate the questioning about our lives and they will take charge of our *ruh* (soul).

How will they carry our souls away?

This depends upon how you lived your lives. Whether you attended unflinchingly to your *salah*, upheld the five pillars, avoided *shirk* and remained constant in the performance of good deeds and in the avoidance of bad deeds.

So, if we neglected our duties towards Allah, we can expect rough treatment from the *malaika* after our death?

Yes. It is *malaika* who take the souls of the wicked initially and lead those very souls to *Jahannam* (Hellfire). The Qur'aan describes this.

وَلَوْ تَرَىٰٓ إِذْ يَتَوَفَّى ٱلَّذِينَ كَفَرُوٓاْ ٱلْمَلَٰٓئِكَةُ يَضْرِبُونَ

وُجُوهَهُمْ وَأَدْبَٰرَهُمْ وَذُوقُواْ عَذَابَ ٱلْحَرِيقِ ۝

And if you could see when the angels take the souls of those who disbelieved.... They are striking their faces and their backs [saying], "Taste the punishment of the burning fire." (Soorah al Anfaal; 8:50).

It is *malaika* who stand guard over the wicked in *Jahannam*. They are cruel, stern and rough acting strictly in accordance with Allah's command:

يَٰٓأَيُّهَا ٱلَّذِينَ ءَامَنُواْ قُوٓاْ أَنفُسَكُمْ وَأَهْلِيكُمْ نَارًا وَقُودُهَا ٱلنَّاسُ

وَٱلْحِجَارَةُ عَلَيْهَا مَلَٰٓئِكَةٌ غِلَاظٌ شِدَادٌ لَّا يَعْصُونَ ٱللَّهَ مَآ أَمَرَهُمْ وَيَفْعَلُونَ

مَا يُؤْمَرُونَ ۝

O you who have believed! Protect yourselves and your families from a Fire whose fuel is people and stones over which are [appointed] angels, harsh and severe; they do not disobey Allah in what He commands them to do, but do what they are commanded. (Soorah at Tahreem; 66:6)

What about those who had remained obedient throughout their lives?

The words from the *malaika* for them are sweet and beautiful expressions of welcome:

جَنَّتُ عَدْنٍ يَدْخُلُونَهَا وَمَن صَلَحَ مِنْ ءَابَآبِهِمْ وَأَزْوَٰجِهِمْ وَذُرِّيَّٰتِهِمْ وَٱلْمَلَٰٓئِكَةُ يَدْخُلُونَ عَلَيْهِم مِّن كُلِّ بَابٍ ۞ سَلَٰمٌ عَلَيْكُم بِمَا صَبَرْتُمْ فَنِعْمَ عُقْبَى ٱلدَّارِ ۞

Gardens of perpetual residence: they will enter them with whoever was righteous among their fathers, their spouses and their descendents. And the angels will enter upon them from every gate [saying] "Peace be upon you for what you patiently endured. And excellent is the final home." (Soorah ar Ra'd; 13:23-24)

Will angels be able to help us on the day of Judgement?

No. Not unless Allah Wills. Despite His immense love for them, on that Day the *malaika* will remain humble and silent before Allah. They will not be able to speak on our behalf, unless Allah grants permission.

۞ وَكَم مِّن مَّلَكٍ فِى ٱلسَّمَٰوَٰتِ لَا تُغْنِى شَفَٰعَتُهُمْ شَيْئًا إِلَّا مِنْ بَعْدِ أَن يَأْذَنَ ٱللَّهُ لِمَن يَشَآءُ وَيَرْضَىٰٓ ۞

How many angels there are in the heavens whose intercession will not avail at all except [only] after Allah has permitted [it] to whom He wills and approves. (Soorah an Najm; 53:26)

If we remain obedient servants of Allah, we can expect their words of comfort:

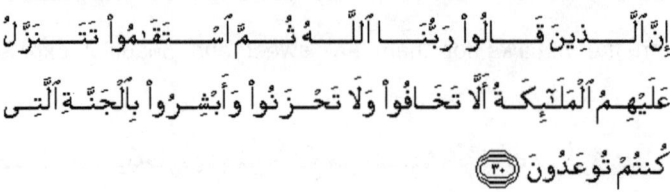

Indeed, thoe who have said, "Our Lord is Allah" and then remained on a right course - the angels will descend upon them, [saying], "Do not fear and do not grieve! but receive good tidings of Paradise which you were promised! (Soorah Fussilat; 41:30)

If we attend salah in jamaah, we can expect their dua's of forgiveness:

Abu Huraira narrates that the Prophet sallallahu alayhe wasalam said, "The prayer offered in congregation is twenty five times more superior (in reward) to the prayer offered alone in one's house or in a business center, because if one performs ablution and does it perfectly, and then proceeds to the mosque with the sole intention of praying, then for each step which he takes towards the mosque, Allah upgrades him a degree in reward and (forgives) crosses out one sin till he enters the mosque. When he enters the mosque he is considered in prayer as long as he is waiting for the prayer and the angels keep on asking for Allah's forgiveness for him and they keep on saying: 'O Allah! Be Merciful to him, O Allah! Forgive him, as long as he keeps on sitting at his praying place and does not pass wind. (Sahih Bukhari; 1:466)

We can expect their favourable reports about us back to Allah Subhaan Wa T'ala:

Abu Hurairah narrates that Allah's Apostle sallallahu alayhe wasalam said, "Angels come to you in succession by night and day and all of them get together at the time of the Fajr and 'Asr prayers. Those who have passed the night with you (or stayed with you) ascend (to the Heaven) and Allah asks them, though He knows everything about you, well, "In what state did you leave my slaves?" The angels reply: "When we left them they were praying and when we reached them, they were praying." (Sahih Bukhari; 1:503)

We can acquire forgiveness of our sins if our voices coincide with theirs when saying "Ameen"

Abu Hurairah narrates that Allah's Apostle sallallahu alayhe wasalam said, "If any one of you says, 'Amin' and the angels in the heavens say 'Amin' and the former coincides with the latter, all his past sins will be forgiven." (Sahih Bukhari; 1:748)

If we are careful we can expect them in our houses:

Abu Talha narrates, I heard Allah's Apostle sallallahu alayhe wasalam saying; "Angels (of Mercy) do not enter a house wherein there is a dog or a picture of a living creature (a human being or an animal)." (Sahih Bukhari)

We can expect, InshAllah, rewards equivalent to animal sacrificing if they note us attending Jum'ah salah early:

Abu Hurairah narrates that Allah's Apostle sallallahu alayhe wasalam said , "When it is a Friday, the angels stand at the gate of the mosque and keep on writing the names of the persons coming to the mosque in succession according to their arrivals. The example of the one who enters the mosque in the earliest hour is that of one offering a camel (in sacrifice). The one coming next is like one offering a cow and then a ram and then a chicken and then an egg respectively. When the Imam comes out (for Jumua prayer) they (i.e. angels) fold their papers and listen to the Khutba." (Sahih Bukhari; 2:51)

REMEMBER ALLAH ALWAYS, STAY IN GOOD COMPANY, INCLUDING THE COMPANY OF THE *MALAIKA*

CHAPTER SIX

Can I ask about Al Kutub [The Books]?

These are the Books of Allah. They are the direct Word of Allah given to mankind to guide and instruct them in following the straight path. They were sent down to earth to Allah's messengers, to help them convey the message of Islaam.

What do you mean by "messengers"?

These were people sent to every community to tell men and women about Islaam and, amongst other things,:

- To exhort them towards *tawheed*;
- To inform them about Allah and *al ghaib*;
- To tell them about the purpose of their creation;
- To instruct them in the *shari'ah* (Divine Legislation);
- To warn them of the consequences of doing bad;
- To remind them of the great rewards in store for doing good;
- To teach them how to live their lives in peace, harmony and with justice for all.

Another name for them is *nabi*, (Prophet – plural, *anbiya*)[1].

So, by sending Books, Allah helped these messengers to fulfil their missions?

Yes. The *anbiya* were very capable people. They performed their task of *da'wah* by speaking to all around them, by setting excellent standards of behaviour and by the performance, with the Help of Allah, of miracles.

---

[1] We will look more closely at the *anbiya* in chapter eight, Insh'Allah.

However, to strengthen them further, Allah gave four of the *anbiya* Books. He says:

لَقَدْ أَرْسَلْنَا رُسُلَنَا بِالْبَيِّنَتِ وَأَنزَلْنَا مَعَهُمُ الْكِتَبَ وَالْمِيزَانَ
لِيَقُومَ النَّاسُ بِالْقِسْطِ

We have already sent our messengers with clear evidences and sent down with them the Scripture and the Balance [of Right and Wrong] that the people may maintain [their affairs] in justice; (Soorah al Hadeed; 57:25)

Who were the four *anbiya* who received Books? What are the names of those books?

The four *anbiya* were:

1. Musa alayhe salam (Moses)

He received the *Towrah* (Torah or Old Testament).

ثُمَّ ءَاتَيْنَا مُوسَى الْكِتَبَ تَمَامًا عَلَى الَّذِيَ أَحْسَنَ وَتَفْصِيلًا
لِّكُلِّ شَيْءٍ وَهُدًى وَرَحْمَةً لَّعَلَّهُم بِلِقَاءِ رَبِّهِمْ يُؤْمِنُونَ ۝

Then [additionally or moreover] We gave Moses the Scripture, making complete [Our favour] upon the one who did good [i.e. Moses] as a detailed explanation of all things and as a guidance and mercy that perhaps in the meeting with their Lord they would believe. (Soorah Al A'naam; 6-154)

2. Dawood Alayhe Salaam (David)

He received *Zaboor* (The Paslms);

وَءَاتَيْنَا دَاوُودَ زَبُورًا ۝

and to David We gave the book of Psalms. (Soorah Al Israa'; 17:55)

3. Eesa alayhe salaam (Jesus)

He received *Injeel* (The Gospel)

ثُمَّ قَفَّيْنَا عَلَىٰٓ ءَاثَٰرِهِم بِرُسُلِنَا وَقَفَّيْنَا بِعِيسَى ٱبْنِ مَرْيَمَ وَءَاتَيْنَٰهُ

ٱلْإِنجِيلَ وَجَعَلْنَا فِى قُلُوبِ ٱلَّذِينَ ٱتَّبَعُوهُ رَأْفَةً وَرَحْمَةً وَرَهْبَانِيَّةً

Then We sent following their footsteps [i.e. traditions] Our messengers and followed [them] with Jesus the son of Mary and gave him the Gospel; and We placed in the hearts of those who followed him compassion and mercy and monasticism. (Soorah al Hadeed; 57-27)

4. Muhammad sallalahu alayhe wasalam –

He received the Qur'aan

ٱللَّهُ نَزَّلَ أَحْسَنَ ٱلْحَدِيثِ كِتَٰبًا مُّتَشَٰبِهًا مَّثَانِىَ تَقْشَعِرُّ

مِنْهُ جُلُودُ ٱلَّذِينَ يَخْشَوْنَ رَبَّهُمْ ثُمَّ تَلِينُ جُلُودُهُمْ وَقُلُوبُهُمْ

إِلَىٰ ذِكْرِ ٱللَّهِ ذَٰلِكَ هُدَى ٱللَّهِ يَهْدِى بِهِۦ مَن يَشَآءُ وَمَن يُضْلِلِ ٱللَّهُ فَمَا

لَهُۥ مِنْ هَادٍ ۞

Allah has sent down the best statement: a consistent Book wherein is reiteration. The skins shiver therefrom of those who fear their Lord; then their skins and their hearts relax at the rememberance [i.e. mention] of Allah. That is the guidance of Allah by which He guides whom He wills. And one whom He leaves astray – for him there is no guide. (Soorah Az Zumar; 39:23)

Which community of people did Books previous to the Qur'aan[1] come to?

The earlier books (*Towrah, Zaboor* and *Injeel*) came to the specific followers of Moosa, Dawood and Eesa respectively. For example, the *Towrah* was sent to guide the *Bani Israel* (The Children of Israel).

وَءَاتَيْنَا مُوسَى ٱلْكِتَٰبَ وَجَعَلْنَٰهُ هُدًى لِّبَنِىٓ إِسْرَٰٓءِيلَ أَلَّا تَتَّخِذُوا۟

مِن دُونِى وَكِيلًا ۞

---

[1] In this work I will refer to the *Towrah, Zaboor* and *Injeel* as the "previous books" or "the earlier books" – Abu Omar

And We gave Moses the Scripture and made it a Guidance for the Children of Israel that you not take other than Me as Disposer of affairs.[1]" (Soorah al Israa'; 17:2)

The recipients of those three previous books, and the generations after them are described in the Qur'aan as "*Ehle Kitaab*" – People of the Book. This is because they were given revelation from Allah. He tells us in the Qur'aan that (interpretation of the meaning),"…For every term is a Decree [or for each period is a Book (revealed)]."[2]

The final book, The Qur'aan, was not revealed for a particular community or to cover a particular limited period. Rather, it was revealed for ALL of mankind until the Day of Judgement. It was also a book for the *Jinn*, the other creation who inhabit the earth with us.

You mentioned The Old Testament, The Psalms and the Gospel. Aren't they part of the Bible?

Yes. Today they are part of what the Christians and the Jews call the Bible.

So, does that mean, as Muslims, we can follow the Bible?

No. When the *Towrah*, *Zaboor* and *Injeel* first came to earth, they were the original Word of Allah, pure and ulaltered. However, over time, the words and meaning of all these Heavenly Books were changed and then bought together to make up "The Bible." Consequently, the Bible contains many statements and beliefs completely contrary to those originally given by Allah to the prophets.

So, as it stands today, we cannot rely on the Bible as the accurate word of Allah?

No. We cannot.

If we cannot trust the words of today's Bible, why are we required to believe in the Books of Allah, *Towrah*, *Zaboor* and *Injeel*, which themselves are in the Bible? Why bother knowing about those Books at all?

Be careful to distinguish between the original books from Allah as opposed to the versions of these books contained in the Bible today.

Muslims believe in the original *Towrah*, *Zaboor* and *Injeel* as the pure and correct Word of Allah. We do not believe in or follow the changed and corrupted versions of those books as they stand today.

---

[1] i.e. trust in Allah, knowing that He is responsible for every occurrence.
[2] Soorah ar Ra'd; 13:38

Is belief in the Books of Allah an article of faith?

Yes. As Muslims we are required to believe without doubt in the Qur'aan and without doubt, that the pure, original *Towrah*, *Zaboor* and *Injeel* were revealed to Musa, Dawood and Eesa Alayhum salaam. If you deny the Kutoob Allah, you fall outside Islaam and into the realms of *kufr* (disbelief), may Allah preserve us from that. Allah Subhaana says

يَـٰٓأَيُّهَا ٱلَّذِينَ ءَامَنُوٓاْ ءَامِنُواْ بِٱللَّهِ وَرَسُولِهِۦ وَٱلْكِتَـٰبِ ٱلَّذِى نَزَّلَ عَلَىٰ رَسُولِهِۦ وَٱلْكِتَـٰبِ ٱلَّذِىٓ أَنزَلَ مِن قَبْلُ وَمَن يَكْفُرْ بِٱللَّهِ وَمَلَـٰٓئِكَتِهِۦ وَكُتُبِهِۦ وَرُسُلِهِۦ وَٱلْيَوْمِ ٱلْأَخِرِ فَقَدْ ضَلَّ ضَلَـٰلَۢا بَعِيدًا ﴿١٣٦﴾

O you who have believed, believe in Allah and his Messenger and the Book that He has sent down upon His Messenger and the Scripture which He sent down before. And who disbelieves in Allah, His angels, His Books His messengers and the Last Day has certainly gone, far astray. (Soorah an Nisaa'; 4:136)

Tell me about the Qur'aan?

The Qur'aan is the final revelation from Allah. It is His infallible Word revealed to His final Messenger Muhammad sallallahu alayhe wasalam. The Qur'aan abrogates all the Books of Allah that came before it and stands as a witness over them. Allah says:

وَأَنزَلْنَآ إِلَيْكَ ٱلْكِتَـٰبَ بِٱلْحَقِّ مُصَدِّقًا لِّمَا بَيْنَ يَدَيْهِ مِنَ ٱلْكِتَـٰبِ وَمُهَيْمِنًا عَلَيْهِ

And We have revealed to you, [O Muhammad], the Book [i.e. the Qur'aan] in truth confirming that which preceeded it of the Scripture and as a criterion over it. (Soorah Ma'idah; 5:48)

The Qur'aan is like a guardian over the other books. We know that the other books have been changed. In those previous books, it is now difficult to distinguish between those parts that were Divinely revealed and those written by human hand. Those books cannot therefore now be trusted.

Because it is competely accurate and unchanged, the Qur'aan acts as a benchmark by which we can be informed and warned about the fabrication in those previous books.

Why didn't the Qur'aan get changed also?

Alhamdulilah, the road of fabricating Divine Words is one the Muslims did not go down. Any Muslim with *taqwa*[1] would never dare do such a thing, and anyone who tried, would surely fail. Not one dash or dot of the Qur'aan has changed in the 1400 years since its revelation. The Qur'aan is a book protected by Allah:

$$ إِنَّا نَحْنُ نَزَّلْنَا ٱلذِّكْرَ وَإِنَّا لَهُۥ لَحَٰفِظُونَ ٩ $$

Indeed it is We who sent down the message (i.e. The Qur'aan), and indeed, We will be its guardian. (Soorah al Hijr; 15:9)

It is a book preserved both on paper and in the hearts of millions of *huffaadha* (Qur'aanic memorisors) around the world.[2]

Who made the changes to the previous books?

The Jews and the Christians, the People of the Book themselves.

Why did they do this?

They could have made changes for a whole host of reasons:

- Maybe they changed words to settle divisions and disputes amongst themselves.
- Maybe some amongst them were motivated by personal, political or financial gain.
- Maybe there were things in the Words of Allah that were not allowing them to achieve their goals, so, they either added, removed or changed words to suit themselves.

Allah hu 'Alim (Allah Knows Best).

Did they not realise they were tampering with the very words of Allah?

They knew very well what they were doing, but, without any fear of Allah and thinking only of themselves, they continued nonetheless. Allah says of them:

$$ يَـٰٓأَهْلَ ٱلْكِتَـٰبِ لِمَ تَلْبِسُونَ ٱلْحَقَّ بِٱلْبَـٰطِلِ وَتَكْتُمُونَ ٱلْحَقَّ وَأَنتُمْ تَعْلَمُونَ ٧١ $$

---

[1] Piety, fear, consciousness of Allah.

[2] We will, Insh'Allah, discuss the Qur'aan more fully in chapter seven.

O people of the Scripture, why do you mix [i.e. confuse] the truth with falsehood and conceal the truth while you know [it]? (Soorah Aali 'Imraan; 3:71)

What changes were made to the previous books?

Five words sum up why we cannot trust the previous books as they stand today:

- **Adding**
- **Subtracting**
- **Twisting**
- **Changing**
- **Translating**

1. Adding

Parts have been added to earlier scriptures that were never sanctioned by Allah. Allah Ta'aala says:

فَوَيْلٌ لِّلَّذِينَ يَكْتُبُونَ ٱلْكِتَـٰبَ بِأَيْدِيهِمْ ثُمَّ يَقُولُونَ هَـٰذَا مِنْ عِندِ ٱللَّهِ لِيَشْتَرُواْ بِهِۦ ثَمَنًا قَلِيلًا فَوَيْلٌ لَّهُم مِّمَّا كَتَبَتْ أَيْدِيهِمْ وَوَيْلٌ لَّهُم مِّمَّا يَكْسِبُونَ ﴿٧٩﴾

So, woe, to those who write the "scripture" with their own hands then say, "This is from Allah" in order to exchange it for a small price. Woe to them for what their hands have written and woe to them for what they earn. (Soorah al Baqara ~ The Cow; 2:79)

2. Subtracting

Parts that were difficult to bear or that didn't fit into the ideas of the recipients of these books were simply removed altogether. Allah says:

أَمْ تَقُولُونَ إِنَّ إِبْرَٰهِـۧمَ وَإِسْمَـٰعِيلَ وَإِسْحَـٰقَ وَيَعْقُوبَ وَٱلْأَسْبَاطَ كَانُواْ هُودًا أَوْ نَصَـٰرَىٰ قُلْ ءَأَنتُمْ أَعْلَمُ أَمِ ٱللَّهُ وَمَنْ أَظْلَمُ مِمَّن كَتَمَ شَهَـٰدَةً عِندَهُۥ مِنَ ٱللَّهِ وَمَا ٱللَّهُ بِغَـٰفِلٍ عَمَّا تَعْمَلُونَ ﴿١٤٠﴾

Or do you say that Abraham and Ishmael and Isaac and Jacob the Descendants were Jews or Christians? Say, "Are you more knowing or is Allah?" And who is more unjust than one who conceals a testimony he has from Allah. And Allah is not unaware of what you do. (Soorah al Baqarah; 2:140)

Sometimes material gain could be acquired by removing Allah's Words. He says:

$$إِنَّ ٱلَّذِينَ يَكْتُمُونَ مَا أَنزَلَ ٱللَّهُ مِنَ ٱلْكِتَـٰبِ وَيَشْتَرُونَ بِهِۦ ثَمَنًا قَلِيلًا$$

$$أُوْلَـٰٓئِكَ مَا يَأْكُلُونَ فِى بُطُونِهِمْ إِلَّا ٱلنَّارَ وَلَا يُكَلِّمُهُمُ ٱللَّهُ يَوْمَ ٱلْقِيَـٰمَةِ وَلَا$$

$$يُزَكِّيهِمْ وَلَهُمْ عَذَابٌ أَلِيمٌ ﴿١٧٤﴾$$

Indeed they who conceal what Allah has sent down of the Book and exchange it for a small price, they consume not into their bellies except the Fire. And Allah will not speak to them on the Day of Resurrection nor will He purify them; And they will have a painful punishment. (Soorah al Baqarah; 2:174)

3. Twisting

The people of the earlier books inferred their own meanings into Allah's words:

$$وَإِنَّ مِنْهُمْ لَفَرِيقًا يَلْوُۥنَ أَلْسِنَتَهُم بِٱلْكِتَـٰبِ لِتَحْسَبُوهُ مِنَ ٱلْكِتَـٰبِ وَمَا$$

$$هُوَ مِنَ ٱلْكِتَـٰبِ وَيَقُولُونَ هُوَ مِنْ عِندِ ٱللَّهِ وَمَا هُوَ مِنْ عِندِ ٱللَّهِ$$

$$وَيَقُولُونَ عَلَى ٱللَّهِ ٱلْكَذِبَ وَهُمْ يَعْلَمُونَ ﴿٧٨﴾$$

And indeed, there is among them a party who alter the Scripture with their tongues so you may think it is from the Scripture, but it is not from the Scripture. And they say, "This is from Allah," but it is not from Allah. And they speak untruth about Allah while they know. (Soorah Aali Imraan ~ The Family of Imraan; 3:78)

So for their breaking of the covenant We cursed them and made their hearts hard. They distort words from their (proper) places (i.e. usages) and have forgotten a portion of that which they were reminded.[1] (Soorah al Maa'idah; 5:13)[2]

---

[1] In the Towrah concerning the coming of Prophet Muhammad *sallallahu alayhe wasallam*

[2] Ibn Kathir comments on the line *"They change the words from their (right) places"* saying, "it means that they play havoc with the words of Allah and misinterpret His Book, taking it to mean things that were never meant and attributing to Allah things that He never said; May Allah protect us from that." [*Tafseer Ibn Katheer*]

4. Changing

أَفَتَطْمَعُونَ أَن يُؤْمِنُواْ لَكُمْ وَقَدْ كَانَ فَرِيقٌ مِّنْهُمْ يَسْمَعُونَ كَلَـٰمَ ٱللَّهِ

ثُمَّ يُحَرِّفُونَهُۥ مِنۢ بَعْدِ مَا عَقَلُوهُ وَهُمْ يَعْلَمُونَ ۝

Do you covet [the hope O believers], that they would believe for you while a party of them (Jewish Rabbis) used to hear the Word of Allaah (the Tawraat), and then distort it after they had understood it while they were knowing? (Soorah al Baqarah; 2:75)

The *aalim* Qutaadah said: "The phrase 'then they used to change it knowingly after they understood it' refers to the Jews, who used to hear the words of Allah, then they altered it after they had understood what it meant."

Many of the commandments of Allah remain intact even today in the Bible, but in a secular environment, they are simply and conveniently ignored and forgotten by today's *Ehle Kitaab.*[1] Allah warns them about this:

قُلْ يَـٰٓأَهْلَ ٱلْكِتَـٰبِ لَسْتُمْ عَلَىٰ شَىْءٍ حَتَّىٰ تُقِيمُواْ ٱلتَّوْرَىٰةَ

وَٱلْإِنجِيلَ وَمَآ أُنزِلَ إِلَيْكُم مِّن رَّبِّكُمْ

Say, "O People of the Scripture, you are (standing) on nothing until you uphold (the law of) the *Towrah*, the Gospel and what has been revealed to you from your Lord[2]." (Soorah al Ma'idah; 5:68)

5. Translating

The earlier books have been translated, edited and revised beyond all recognition. We do not know what the original *Towrah*, *Zaboor* and *Injeel* have to say because they are not available today in their original languages, namely the languages of Musa, Dawood and Eesa alayhum salaam. Did Jesus, the son of Mary, speak the language of King James? Was Musa alay salaam fluent in Latin or Greek? Clearly not!

Translating holy scripture into other languages is extremely dangerous. Even innocent reinterpretation can alter or even destroy the original message

---

[1] The prohibition of interest in business affairs and the ban on the consumption of alcohol are just two of many examples.
[2] i.e. The Qur'aan

But I have seen translations of the Qur'aan in so many languages.

Alhamdulilah the Qur'aan has now been translated into many many languages. That is great and those translations will help millions to understand Allah's Book as they must. Allah says (interpretation of the meaning), "Those to whom We have sent the book study it as it should be studied."[1]

However, be careful. We cannot call those translations, "The Qur'aan." They are "Interpretations of the Meaning of the Qur'aan", or "Translations of the Meaning of the Qur'aan." Only the Arabic text of our Book can be described as "The Qur'aan."

Consequently, translations cannot be accepted exclusively for reference in matters of theological debate or law or in acts of worship. Whilst they can be referred to, where questions arise, the Arabic text stands as the final arbiter.

So, there are no "versions" of the Qur'aan as is the case (in hundreds) with the Bible?

No, there aren't. Unlike previous books, the Qur'aan is not a collection of writings by multiple human authors generated over thousands of years. It is a revelation from Allah Himself. The Qur'aan today stands in its original glorious form. You will not find the fifth revision of the fourth edition of the Qur'aan. You will not find the King Omar Version or the Grand Moroccan Version of the Qur'aan. Its text is unique, consistent and universal.

$$\text{وَٱتْلُ مَآ أُوحِىَ إِلَيْكَ مِن كِتَابِ رَبِّكَ لَا مُبَدِّلَ لِكَلِمَـٰتِهِۦ وَلَن تَجِدَ}$$

$$\text{مِن دُونِهِۦ مُلْتَحَدًا ﴿٢٧﴾}$$

And recite, [O Muhammad], what has been revealed to you of the Book of your Lord: There is no changer of His Words, and never will you find in other than Him, a refuge. (Soorah al Kahf; 18:27)

The Qur'aan is still in its original Arabic, Alhamdulilah.

Yes. As well as confirming the authenticity of our Holy Book, the Arabic also helps keep our faith vibrant and genuine. Alhamdulilliah, in our *salah*, in our recitation, in all aspects of Islaamic life, the original Arabic is still alive and plays an integral part.

Can we refer to the Bible to discover what kinds of things Allah told the previous prophets?

No. As has been explained, we cannot be sure that anything we read in those books today is accurate. The Qur'aan should be sufficient for all our needs.

---

[1] Soorah Baqarah; 2:121

Muhammad sallallahu alayhe wasalam said, The people of the Scripture (Jews) used to recite the *Towrah* in Hebrew and they used to explain it in Arabic to the Muslims. On that Allah's Apostle said, "Do not believe the people of the Scripture or disbelieve them, but say: "We believe in Allah and what is revealed to us[1]." (Sahih Bukhari; volume 6: *hadith* 12 reported by Abu Hurayrah radhiAllaho anho)

Remember that by delivering Islaam to the world, Allah Ta'aala was completing his favour to His creation. He says:

This day I have perfected for you your religion, and completed my favour upon you and have approved for you Islaam as religion. (Soorah al Ma'idah; 5:3)

When Muhammad sallallahu alayhe wasallam delivered Allah's message to us fourteen hundred years ago, he delivered it in its entirety. By leaving us with the Qur'aan and the Sunnah, he left us with all the tools we need to account for ourselves as Muslims and to pass the message on to others who were not present. As long as we have those two things, then we will never go astray. In his final sermon he said:

I am leaving behind me two things, the Qur'aan and my example, the Sunnah and if you follow these you will never go astray.[2]

Abu Bakr reinforced this point upon the death of the Prophet sallallahu alayhe wasallam:

Narrated Anas bin Malik that he heard Umar radhi Allahu anho speaking (while standing on the pulpit of the Prophet sallallahu alayhe wasallam) in the morning (following the death of the Prophet sallallahu alayhe wasallam), when the people had given Bai'a (pledge) to Abu Bakr. He said the Tashah-hud before Abu Bakr, and added, Amma Badu (then after), Allah has chosen for His Messenger sallallahu alayhe wasallam what is with Him (Paradise) rather than what is with you (the World). This is that Book, (the Qur'aan) with which Allah guided your Messenger, so stick to it, for then you will be guided on the Right Path as Allah guided His Messenger sallallahu alayhe wasallam with it. (Sahih Bukhari ~ vol. 9; *hadith* 374)

---

[1] The quote is verse 2:136 of the Qur'aan.

[2] Related in Ibn Hishaam ~ 2;603, also by Ibn Ishaaq and in Sahih Muslim vol. 2; *hadith* 263

CHAPTER SEVEN

Can I ask about Al Qur'aan

What does the word "Qur'aan" mean?

Literally, it means "recitation" or "reading." It's root lies in the verb "*qara*" (to read).

How did the Qur'aan get its name?

Allah Himself mentions this name multiple times in the Qur'aan itself. For example:

$$كِـتَـٰبٌ فُصِّلَـتۡ ءَايَـٰتُـهُۥ قُرۡءَانًا عَرَبِيًّا لِّقَـوۡمٖ يَعۡلَمُونَ ۝$$

A Book whose verses have been detailed, an Arabic Qur'aan for people who know (Soorah al Fussilat; 41:3)

Does the Qur'aan carry any other names?

Yes. The Qur'aan is variously called:

- *Al Furqaan* (the Criterion to help distinguish between right and wrong – 25:1);
- *Kitaab Allah* (The Book of Allah – 2:1,2);
- *Al Ilm* (The Knowledge – 2:145);
- *Al Hudaa* (The Guidance – 2:2);
- *Bayaan* (The Declaration of the Truth – 3:138);
- *An Nur* (The Light – 4:4);
- *Al Hakeem* (The Wise – 10:1);
- *Al Maw'uzaat* (The Complete Exhortation – 10:57);

- *Al Balagh* (The Clear Message – 14:52);
- *Al Shifa* (The remedy for all spiritual diseases – 17:82);
- *Hubal-Allah* (The Rope of Allah – 3:103);
- *Tanzeel* (the Final Revelation – 39:23);
- *Hikmah* (Divine Words of Wisdom – 65:6);
- *Al Dhikr* (A Constant Reminder – 21:50);
- *Al Amr* (The Commandment – 69:48);
- *Tadhkirah* (A Warrant for the Believer – 43:1,2)

Those are a lot of very descriptive names. It seems the Qur'aan has great relevance?

- Every word of the Qur'aan is a word of profound relevance;
- Its pages contain volumes of inspiration and information;
- In the Qur'aan you can read of the lives of prophets and the fate of past generations;
- You can understand precisely the nature of faith, *tawheed* and obedience to one supreme creator;
- You can be privy to knowledge in the realms of the unseen;
- You can gauge accurately the right path as opposed to the one of error;
- You can be enlightened in complex legal injunctions and matters relating to personal, social and political etiquette;
- You can have described to you a host of natural and scientific phenomena;
- The Qur'aan is our personal light and guide as well as the primary source for our *Shari'ah*, Islaamic law.

What is the structure of the Qur'aan? Does it have chapters like other books?

Yes. The Qur'aan has 114 chapters in all. Each chapter is called a *soorah*. The *soorahs* are divided themselves into *ayaah*. For ease of reading, it is also divided into thirty sections called *Juz*.

What does the word "*ayaah*" mean?

Commonly *ayaah* is translated as "verse" because essentially that's what they are. However, the literal meaning of *ayaah* is "sign." Each verse of the Qur'aan is a "sign" towards belief in Allah and the unseen, towards *tawheed* and the ultimate truth that is Islaam.

What language is the Qur'aan in?

Arabic. To be more specific, *fus-hah* (Classical Arabic). The language of the Qur'aan is of the purest kind. It is eloquent, clear and highly expressive. It does not compare with *aameeyah* (the colloquial Arabic of today). Allah says,

$$\text{إِنَّا جَعَلْنَـٰهُ قُرْءَٰنًا عَرَبِيًّا لَّعَلَّكُمْ تَعْقِلُونَ ۝}$$

Indeed We have made it an Arabic Qur'aan that you might understand. (Soorah az Zukhruf; 43:3)

Is the Qur'aan the Speech of Allah?

Yes. He says:

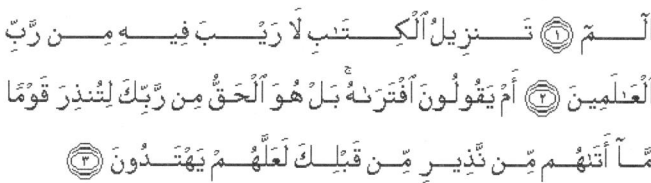

Alif Laam Meem; [This is] the revelation of the Book about which there is no doubt from the Lord of the Worlds. Or do they (the *kuffaar*) say "He [Muhammad sallallahu alayhe wasallam] invented it"? Rather, it is the Truth from the Lord, [O Muhammad], that you may warn a people to whom no warner has come before you [so] perhaps they will be guided. (Soorah as Sajdah; 32:1-3)

So, Muhammad sallallahu alayhe wasallam did not author any part of the Qur'aan?

No. Muhammad sallallahu alayhe wasallam was illiterate.[1] He was certainly an intelligent and cultured man as well as an extremely eloquent speaker. However, he could not read or write, let alone pen such magnificent prose covering so many different themes. In this sense, the Qur'aan is a *mu'awjiza minallah* (a miracle from Allah) and confirms the Prophethood of Muhammad sallallahu alayhe wasallam.

Belief in the miraculous nature of the Qur'aan, is an article of faith in Islaam. Anyone who refutes or doubts that the Qur'aan is the Word of Allah or ascribes authorship to any other person, including Muhammad sallallahu alayhe wasallam, has fallen outside the fold of Islaam. The Qur'aan is a divinely revealed book, sent down to Muhammad sallallahu alayhe wasallam by *wahy zaahir* (manifest inspiration).

What is *wahy zaahir* (manifest inspiration)?

Muhammad sallallahu alayhe wasallam was a Prophet of Allah. All his spoken words were words and concepts inspired to him by Allah. Such inspiration is known as *wahy*.

---

[1] In fact he was known as *al nabi al ummi* [the illiterate prophet]

The Qur'aan notes (interpretation of the meaning), "He [Muhammad sallallahu alayhe wasallam] does not speak from his own accord, rather it is revelation that is revealed." (Soorah an Najm; 53:3-4)

The general words of Muhammad sallallahu alayhe wasallam were based upon *wahy baatin* (internal inspiration). Muhammad sallallahu alayhe wasallam would be inspired about general concepts from Allah and thereafter he would express those concepts to the *sahaabah*. These words formed the *ahadith*.

The Qur'aan was revealed to Muhammad sallallahu alayhe wasallam in a different manner, not by *wahy baatin* but by *wahy zaahir*. Here he would not receive "general concepts", but rather "precise words". These words were the words of the Qur'aan.

During *wahy zaahir*, did Muhammad sallallahu alayhe wasallam hear Allah's own voice?

No. The words of the Qur'aan were delivered to him by the angel Jibra'ee*l*. So, to summarise, *wahy zaahir* is the reciting of the exact words of the Qur'aan through the angel Jibra'eel to Muhammad sallallahu alayhe wasallam. The Qur'aan was always received by *wahy zaahir* (manifest inspiration).

Did Muhammad sallallahu alayhe wasallam know when he was receiving an *ayaah* of the Qur'aan?

Yes. *Wahy zaahir* was very clear to him. When it occurred, he knew that this will not be just a concept to be told to others. These are words that must be incorporated into the Qur'aan. *Wahy zaahir* in this manner happened anywhere. In the mosque, at home, even riding on a camel. Often, people around Muhammad sallallahu alayhe wasallam noticed that he was experiencing *wahy zaahir*, and was listening to the words of *Jibra'eel*.

When was the first occasion of *wahy zaahir*? What I mean, is when did Muhammad sallallahu alayhe wasallam receive his first revelation of the Qur'aan?

Muhammad sallallahu alayhe wasallam received the first revelation of the Qur'aan at the age of forty, from the angel *Jibra'eel* in a cave in Makkah. The cave is called Hira and is to be found on *Jabbal Noor* (Mountain of Light).

In a cave?

Yes. Muhammad sallallahu alayhe wasallam used to go to this cave regularly to meditate and get away from the distractions of the world. This was even before the Qur'aan was revealed to him and the annunciation of his Prophethood.

One night, at the age of forty, Muhammad sallallahu alayhe wasallam was sitting peacefully in the darkness of Hira, when a voice spoke to him. The voice said READ! The voice was that of the angel *Jibra'eel*. Muhammad sallallahu alayhe wasallam was illiterate and so he replied "I cannot read."

Jibra'eel caught hold of Muhammad sallallahu alayhe wasallam, gave him a tight bear hug, released him and repeated again, "READ!" Muhammad sallallahu alayhe wasallam replied again, "I cannot read."

Jibra'eel pressed Muhammad sallallahu alayhe wasallam a second time until he could bear it nomore. He released him and said again in a much stronger voice, "READ!" Muhammad sallallahu alayhe wasallam replied again, "I cannot read?"

Jibra'eel squeezed him again and then proceeded to recite the following[1]:
> *Read! in the name of thy Lord and Cherisher Who created; Created man out of a (mere) clot of congealed blood; Read! And thy Lord is Most Bountiful; Who taught by (the use of) the Pen; Taught man that which he knew not.*

That seems frightening? Was Muhammad sallallahu alayhe wasallam scared?

Yes he was. He ran home, trembling all over with fear. He went to his wife, Khadija radhiAllaho anha and asked her, "cover me, cover me!" She covered him with a blanket until his fear subsided. Muhammad sallallahu alayhe wasallam then told her everything that had happened.

Did she believe him?

Yes. This was such a bizarre story, but Khadija accepted it completely and believed her husband without reservation. This is one of the reasons why Khadija radhiAllaho anha is remembered as a great woman in Islaam.

The next day, Khadija went with Muhammad sallallahu alayhe wasallam to see her cousin Waraqa bin Nawfal. He was a learned person and someone who could possibly interpret the event that had taken place. Waraqa correctly confirmed that the visitor in the cave was an angel and that Muhammad sallallahu alayhe wasallam was the final messenger of Allah, as foretold in previous scriptures.

The Qur'aan mentions the Night of Qadr (*Layla tul Qadr*). Is this the night in Hira?

No. It is the night when the Qur'aan first descended in its entirety from *Lauh al Mahfhoodh* (the preserved tablet), where it was kept with Allah, down to the first heaven, to a place called *Bayt al Izza* (The House of Honour). It was only from here

---

[1] What are today *ayaah* number 1-5 of Surah al Alaqa (96; 1-5) in the Holy Qur'aan

that it was gradually revealed to Muhammad sallallahu alayhe wasallam over twenty-three years.

Did Muhammad sallallahu alayhe wasallam receive regular *ayaahs* after that?

Jibr'aeel would come to Muhammad sallallahu alayhe wasallam with varying frequency and with *ayaahs* of differing quantity and differing lengths.

How many years separated the first and last revelations?

Twenty-three years. Muhammad sallallahu alayhe wasallam was forty years old when Jibra'eel came to him in Hira. He was sixty-three when he received the final revelation just before he died.

Was the revelation of the Qur'aan completed or did Muhammad sallallahu alayhe wasallam die before it could all be revealed in its entirety?

The Holy Qur'aan was revealed in full in those twenty-three years. This process of gradual revelation of the Qur'aan is known as *tanjeem*.

What were the benefits of *tanjeem*?

♦ To impart information:

The Qur'aan is a book bursting at the seams with information. It is full of stories, injunctions and phenomena. The Arabs already knew of some of its contents from scriptures of old. However, a sizeable proportion of the detail was new and consequently, it would have been too much to acquire in one go.

♦ To strengthen faith as a source of peace:

The Qur'aan was a balm and a source of peace. The Muslims were made to feel less fearful and calmer about the new way of life being revealed to them. Gradual revelation allowed them to establish Islaam confidently even in the face of abject hostility.

♦ To ease reading and memorisation:

By gradual revelation, the new community of Muslims could study, learn and implement the Qur'aan, verse by verse. It was not an insurmountable obstacle that had to be scaled immediately. Rather, it was a document that could be reviewed and memorized.

♦ To strengthen faith with miraculous answers to questions:

As they arose, Allah answered direct questions relating to aspects of knowledge known only to certain groups e.g. Jewish scholars. Muhammad sallallahu alayhe wasallam could not have known such answers. It confirmed the Qur'aan's divine nature, thereby fortifying the faith of those early followers. Allah says:

$$وَقَالَ ٱلَّذِينَ كَفَرُواْ لَوْلَا نُزِّلَ عَلَيْهِ ٱلْقُرْءَانُ جُمْلَةً وَٰحِدَةً$$

$$كَذَٰلِكَ لِنُثَبِّتَ بِهِۦ فُؤَادَكَ وَرَتَّلْنَٰهُ تَرْتِيلًا ۝$$

And those who disbelieve say, "Why was the Qur'aan not revealed to him (Muhammad sallallahu alayhe wasallam) all at once?" Thus [it is] that We may strengthen thereby your heart, and We spaced it distinctly, And they do not come to you with an example [i.e. an argument], except that We bring you the Truth and the best explanation. (Soorah al Furqaan; 25:32-33)

♦ **To deal with arguments, challenges and questions as they arose:**

The very *ayaah* mentioned above demonstrates this point. A question would often be set by the unbelievers to whom Allah would directly reveal the answer. The believers also had their own questions answered by the direct revelation of *ayaah* of the Qur'aan.

This contemporaneous provision of answers to questions is a major feature of the Qur'aan, and acts as guide for future generations.

♦ **To change beliefs:**

The Arabs were a people steeped in *al jahaliyah* (The age of ignorance). They had become idolaters using the very sanctuary built by Ibrahim alayhe salaam for the performance of all sorts of bizarre pagan rituals. Idolatry was passed on from generation to generation and had become deeply ingrained in their psyche. Gradual revelation was the easiest way to change this.

♦ **To change behaviour:**

The Arabs were divided kith against kin, tribe against tribe. They broke their pledges and behaved grotesquely in ways, which they justified with words like honour and tradition. They were burying alive new born girls, the sanctity of marriage was in tatters and debauchery and drunkenness were the order of the day.

By contrast, the ultimate standard required of a Muslim was one of discipline and forbearance through charity and prayer. It required physical, spiritual and economic allegiance to one supreme god, Allah. A change from one state to another could best be achieved by gradual revelation.

CHAPTER EIGHT

Can I ask about Ar Rusul [The Messengers]?

Who are Allah's *Rusul*?

They were the Prophets of Allah. They were men who lived on earth, sent by Allah to guide mankind towards submission to His Will. "*Rusul*" is the plural form of the word "*Rasool*." *Rasool* means "the sent one", from the verb "*Arsala*", He sent.

But I thought "*Rasool*" means Messenger, not Prophet?

Strictly speaking, you are correct. There is a difference between these two terms. The consensus among the *ulema* is that a "*Rasool*" is a Messenger who was given a Divine Law (or a Book), whereas a "*Nabi*" (Prophet) is one upon whom no book was given. Ibn Taymiyyah stated, "The correct view is that the Messenger is one who is sent to a disbelieving people, and the Prophet is one who is sent to a believing people with the sharee'ah of the Messenger who came before him, to teach them and judge between them, as Allaah says (interpretation of the meaning), *"Verily, We did send down the Tawraat (Torah) [to Moosa (Moses)], therein was guidance and light, by which the Prophets, who submitted themselves to Allaah's Will, judged for the Jews"* [Soorah al-Maa'idah 5:44]"

However, the word being used in the Pillars of Faith (*Rusul*)[1] covers both Prophets and Messengers. We are required to believe in all those individuals sent by Allah to guide mankind, whether they came with a divine code or not.

---

[1] I believe in Allah and His angels, and his Books, and His Messengers (Rusulihi).....

How many Prophets were there?

There have many, many Prophets since Allah's creation of the earth. Only Allah knows the real number. But one thing is for sure. There has never been a community that was not sent a Prophet to warn them.

$$وَلَقَدْ بَعَثْنَا فِى كُلِّ أُمَّةٍ رَّسُولًا أَنِ اعْبُدُواْ
اللَّهَ وَاجْتَنِبُواْ الطَّغُوتَ$$

"And certainly, We sent into every *Ummah* [nation] a messenger, [saying],: 'Worship Allaah, and avoid *Taaghoo't*'" (Soorah an-Nahl 16:36)

Who was the first Prophet ever?

The first Prophet was also the first man on earth, Aadam alayhe salaam (Adam – peace be upon him).

And Muhammad sallallahu alayhe wasalam was the last?

Yes. Allah says

$$مَّا كَانَ مُحَمَّدٌ أَبَآ أَحَدٍ مِّن رِّجَالِكُمْ وَلَـٰكِن رَّسُولَ اللَّهِ وَخَاتَمَ النَّبِيِّـۧنَ
وَكَانَ اللَّهُ بِكُلِّ شَىْءٍ عَلِيمًا ﴿﴾$$

Muhammad is not the father of [any] one of your men but [he is] the Messenger of Allah and the seal [i.e. the last] of the Prophets: and ever is Allah of all things Knowing. (Soorah al Ahzaab; 33:40)

He is absolutely the last ever?

Yes. No more Prophets were sent after Muhammad sallallahu alayhe wasalam and none will be sent in the future. He is the Messenger for all mankind and *jinn* until Yawm al Qiyamah (The Day of Judgement). He himself said, *"There will be no Prophet after me,"*[2]

---

[1] false objects of worship.
[2] Sahih Bukhari; 4:661, narrated by Abu Hurairah

Is it a sin to believe that another Prophet will come after Muhammad sallallahu alayhe wasalam?

It is more than a sin. If you believe that other Prophets followed Muhammad sallallahu alayhe wasalam or are due to follow him in the future, you fall outside the pale of Islaam and become a *kaafir*, May Allah preserve us from that.

Are all the many Prophets mentioned in the Qur'aan?

Allah tells us that many Prophets were sent but that He has only mentioned a few in His Book:

$$وَرُسُـــلًا قَـــدْ قَصَصْنَـٰهُـــمْ عَلَيۡـــكَ مِـــن قَبۡـــلُ وَرُسُـــلًا لَّـــمْ نَقۡصُصۡهُـــمْ عَلَيۡـــكَ$$

And [We sent] messengers about whom We have related [their stories] to you before and messengers about whom We have not related to you. (Soorah an Nisaa'; 4:164)

How many Prophets does the Qur'aan mentions?

Twenty-five. They are:

1. **Aadam, alayhe salam[1] (Adam)**
2. **Idrees, alayhe salam**
3. **Nuh, alayhe salam (Noah)**
4. **Hood, alayhe salam**
5. **Saalih,**
6. **Ibraaheem, alayhe salam (Abraham)**
7. **Loot, alayhe salam (Lot)**
8. **Ismaa'eel, alayhe salam (Ishmail)**
9. **Ishaaq, alayhe salam (Isaac)**
10. **Ya'qoob, alayhe salam (Jacob)**
11. **Yoosuf, alayhe salam (Joseph)**
12. **Shu'ayb, alayhe salam**
13. **Ayyoob, alayhe salam (Job)**
14. **Dhu'l-Kifl, alayhe salam**
15. **Moosa, alayhe salam (Moses)**
16. **Haaroon, (Aaron)**
17. **Dawood, alayhe salam (David)**

---

[1] "Alayhe salaam" means "Peace be upon him" and is a term preferably used when mentioning the names of Prophets.

18. **Sulaymaan, alayhe salam (Solomon)**
19. **Ilyaas, alayhe salam (Elias)**
20. **al-Yasa', (Elisha)**
21. **Yoonus, alayhe salam (Jonah)**
22. **Zakariyya, alayhe salam (Zacharias)**
23. **Yahyaa, alayhe salam (John)**
24. **'Eesa alayhe salam (Jesus)**
25. **Muhammad sallallahu alayhe wasalam**

What language did the Prophets speak in?

The Prophets were sent to different nations at different times. They were often born and grew up in the nations in which they preached. They knew the customs and languages of those nations. This was so that the message of Islaam could be given clearly to the people being spoken to. The Qur'aan mentions:

$$\text{وَمَآ أَرْسَلْنَا مِن رَّسُولٍ إِلَّا بِلِسَانِ قَوْمِهِۦ}$$

And we did not send any messenger except [speaking] in the language of his people to state clearly for them. (Soorah Ibraheem; 14:4)

What kind of things did the Prophets preach?

Before I answer that, I want you to tell me what <u>you</u> think was the most important lesson preached by the Prophets?

It must be *tawheed*.

Yes. This is the first thing you must know about the Message of the Messengers of Allah. They ALL preached *tawheed*. They all instructed and guided their people towards the worship of One God.

ALL the Prophets did this?

Yes. All of them without exception.

$$\text{لَقَدْ أَرْسَلْنَا نُوحًا إِلَىٰ قَوْمِهِۦ فَقَالَ يَـٰقَوْمِ اعْبُدُواْ اللَّهَ مَا لَكُم مِّنْ إِلَـٰهٍ}$$
$$\text{غَيْرُهُۥٓ إِنِّىٓ أَخَافُ عَلَيْكُمْ عَذَابَ يَوْمٍ عَظِيمٍ ﴿٥٩﴾}$$

We had certainly sent Noah to his people, and he said, "O my people! worship Allah! you have no deity other than Him. Indeed I fear for you the punishment of a tremendous Day! (Soorah A'raaf; 7:59)

أَمْ كُنتُمْ شُهَدَاءَ إِذْ حَضَرَ يَعْقُوبَ ٱلْمَوْتُ إِذْ قَالَ لِبَنِيهِ مَا

تَعْبُدُونَ مِنْ بَعْدِى قَالُواْ نَعْبُدُ إِلَٰهَكَ وَإِلَٰهَ ءَابَآئِكَ إِبْرَٰهِۦمَ

وَإِسْمَٰعِيلَ وَإِسْحَٰقَ إِلَٰهًا وَٰحِدًا وَنَحْنُ لَهُۥ مُسْلِمُونَ ﴿١٣٣﴾

Or were you witnesses when death approached Jacob? When he said to his sons: "What will you worship after me?" They said: "We shall worship your God and the God of your fathers, Abraham Ishmael and Isaac - One God. And we are Muslims [in submission] to Him." (Soorah al Baqarah; 2:133)

۞ وَإِلَىٰ ثَمُودَ أَخَاهُمْ صَٰلِحًا قَالَ يَٰقَوْمِ ٱعْبُدُواْ ٱللَّهَ مَا لَكُم

مِّنْ إِلَٰهٍ غَيْرُهُۥ

To the Thamood [We sent] their brother Salih. He said: "O my people! worship Allah: you have no deity other than Him. (Soorah Hood; 11:61)

وَٱتَّبَعْتُ مِلَّةَ ءَابَآئِى إِبْرَٰهِيمَ وَإِسْحَٰقَ وَيَعْقُوبَ مَا كَانَ لَنَآ أَن نُّشْرِكَ

بِٱللَّهِ مِن شَىْءٍ ذَٰلِكَ مِن فَضْلِ ٱللَّهِ عَلَيْنَا وَعَلَى ٱلنَّاسِ وَلَٰكِنَّ أَكْثَرَ ٱلنَّاسِ

لَا يَشْكُرُونَ ﴿٣٨﴾

"And I[1] have followed the religion of my fathers Abraham Isaac and Jacob; and it was not for us to associate anything with Allah. That is from the favour of Allah upon us and upon the people, but most of the people are not grateful. (Soorah Yoosuf; 12:38)

Did they tolerate idolatry in order maybe to convey the general message?

No. Never. They NEVER tolerated idolatry in any form. They always spoke against it and made it's evil very clear to their people. Even Ibraheem told his own father of its evil:

---

[1] Yousuf alayhe salam is speaking here in jail to fellow prisoners

78

$$\Leftrightarrow وَإِذْ قَالَ إِبْرَاهِيمُ لِأَبِيهِ ءَازَرَ أَتَتَّخِذُ أَصْنَامًا ءَالِهَةً إِنِّي أَرَىٰكَ وَقَوْمَكَ$$

$$فِي ضَلَالٍ مُّبِينٍ ﴿٧٤﴾$$

And [mention, O Muhammad], when Abraham said to his father Aazar, Do you take idols for deities? Indeed I see you and your people to be in manifest error." (Soorah al An'aam; 6:74)

OK, so *tawheed* was the primary message. What other messages did they preach?

- Information about Allah and *al ghaib* (the unseen);
- Guidance about the purpose of our creation;
- Legal codes ~ the *shari'ah*;
- Moral guidance;
- Warnings about specific events to befall the community;
- Reminders of the rewards for doing good;
- Warnings about the consequence of doing bad.

So no one can say on *Yawm Al Qiyaamah*, "I did not receive the message?"

Yes. No one can say, *"How can I be punished? A warner was not sent to me!"* Allah has sent a warner to every nation.

$$رُّسُلًا مُّبَشِّرِينَ وَمُنذِرِينَ لِئَلَّا يَكُونَ لِلنَّاسِ عَلَى ٱللَّهِ حُجَّةٌ بَعْدَ$$

$$ٱلرُّسُلِ وَكَانَ ٱللَّهُ عَزِيزًا حَكِيمًا ﴿١١٥﴾$$

[We sent] messengers as bringers of good tidings and warners so that mankind will have no argument against Allah after the messengers. And Allah is ever Exalted in Might and Wise. (Soorah an Nisaa'; 4:165)

Allah is not unjust. He will never punish a people without warning them first.

Were all the Prophets followed by their people?

No. The response from the communities receiving Prophets varied:

$$وَلَقَدْ بَعَثْنَا فِي كُلِّ أُمَّةٍ رَّسُولًا أَنِ ٱعْبُدُواْ$$

$$ٱللَّهَ وَٱجْتَنِبُواْ ٱلطَّاغُوتَ فَمِنْهُم مَّنْ هَدَى ٱللَّهُ وَمِنْهُم مَّنْ حَقَّتْ$$

$$عَلَيْهِ ٱلضَّلَالَةُ$$

79

And We certainly sent into every nation a messenger [saying], "Worship Allah and avoid *taaghoot.*" And among them were those whom Allah guided and among them were those upon whom error was [deservedly] decreed. (Soorah an Nahl; 16:36)

Did any community ever mistreat a Prophet?

Yes. Often. They were rejected, abused and ridiculed by many amongst their communities. Many of them were even killed. Allah tells us about the *Bani Isra'eel* (The Children of Israel led by Moses):

$$لَقَـدْ أَخَذْنَـا مِيثَـٰقَ بَنِـىٓ إِسْـرَٰٓءِيلَ وَأَرْسَـلْنَآ إِلَيْهِـمْ رُسُـلًا$$

$$كُلَّمَـا جَـآءَهُمْ رَسُـولٌۢ بِمَـا لَا تَهْـوَىٰٓ أَنفُسُـهُمْ فَرِيقًـا كَذَّبُـواْ$$

$$وَفَرِيقًـا يَقْتُلُـونَ ۝$$

We had already taken the Covenant of the Children of Israel and had sent to them messengers. Whenever there came to them a messenger with what their souls did not desire, a party [of messengers] they denied, and another party they killed. (Soorah Ma'idah; 5:70)

How did the Prophets cope? They must have had a lot of patience.

Sabr (patience and endurance) is one of the greatest characteristics of the Prophets of Allah. They all had *sabr* and needed it to put up with the ignorance and stubborn-mindedness of their communities.

Consider the example of Nuh alayhe salaam (Noah). He stayed among his people for nine hundred and fifty years, encouraging them towards *tawheed*. However, they were steeped in idolatry and ignorance and stubbornly refused to listen. They even put their fingers in their ears.

They put their fingers in their ears? That's so childish. What did Nuh do to persuade them?

He pleaded with them to the point of exhaustion. Finally, he prayed to his Lord to deal with them as He saw fit. As you read the following text of the interpretation of the meaning of the Qur'aan just consider the sheer exasperation faced by Nuh alayhe salaam. Consider whether you could face the taunts, abuse and humiliation he faced here. Yet still, he remains patient and hopeful of Allah's support:

إِنَّآ أَرْسَلْنَا نُوحًا إِلَىٰ قَوْمِهِۦٓ أَنْ أَنذِرْ قَوْمَكَ مِن قَبْلِ أَن يَأْتِيَهُمْ عَذَابٌ أَلِيمٌ ۞ قَالَ يَٰقَوْمِ إِنِّى لَكُمْ نَذِيرٌ مُّبِينٌ ۞ أَنِ ٱعْبُدُوا۟ ٱللَّهَ وَٱتَّقُوهُ وَأَطِيعُونِ ۞ يَغْفِرْ لَكُم مِّن ذُنُوبِكُمْ وَيُؤَخِّرْكُمْ إِلَىٰٓ أَجَلٍ مُّسَمًّى إِنَّ أَجَلَ ٱللَّهِ إِذَا جَآءَ لَا يُؤَخَّرُ لَوْ كُنتُمْ تَعْلَمُونَ ۞ قَالَ رَبِّ إِنِّى دَعَوْتُ قَوْمِى لَيْلًا وَنَهَارًا ۞ فَلَمْ يَزِدْهُمْ دُعَآءِىٓ إِلَّا فِرَارًا ۞ وَإِنِّى كُلَّمَا دَعَوْتُهُمْ لِتَغْفِرَ لَهُمْ جَعَلُوٓا۟ أَصَٰبِعَهُمْ فِىٓ ءَاذَانِهِمْ وَٱسْتَغْشَوْا۟ ثِيَابَهُمْ وَأَصَرُّوا۟ وَٱسْتَكْبَرُوا۟ ٱسْتِكْبَارًا ۞ ثُمَّ إِنِّى دَعَوْتُهُمْ جِهَارًا ۞ ثُمَّ إِنِّىٓ أَعْلَنتُ لَهُمْ وَأَسْرَرْتُ لَهُمْ إِسْرَارًا ۞ فَقُلْتُ ٱسْتَغْفِرُوا۟ رَبَّكُمْ إِنَّهُۥ كَانَ غَفَّارًا ۞

Indeed, We sent Noah to his people, (saying), "Warn your people before there comes to them a painful punishment." He said, "O my people, indeed I am to you a clear warner, (saying), "Worship Allah, fear Him and obey me. He (i.e. Allah) will forgive you your sins and delay you for a specified term. Indeed, the time (set by) Allah, when it comes, will not be delayed, if you only knew."

He said, "My Lord, indeed I invited my people (to truth) night and day. but my invitation increased them not, except in flight (i.e. aversion). And indeed, every time I invited them that You may forgive them, they put their fingers in their ears, covered themselves with their garments, persisted, and were arrogant with (great) arrogance.

Then I invited them publicly. then I announced to them and (also) confided to them secretly. And said, "Ask forgiveness of your Lord. Indeed, He is ever a Perpetual Forgiver. (Soorah Nuh   Noah; 71:1-10)

Did Muhammad sallallahu alayhe wasalam face similar pressures.

Yes. Our beloved Prophet Muhammad sallallahu alayhe wasallam was not spared adversity. Death, danger and difficulties were ever-present companions for Muhammad sallallahu alayhe wasalam and the sahaabah. However, Allah always comforted them with reminders of the hardships endured by the previous Prophets:

الٓمٓ ۝ أَحَسِبَ ٱلنَّاسُ أَن يُتْرَكُوٓاْ أَن يَقُولُوٓاْ ءَامَنَّا وَهُمْ لَا يُفْتَنُونَ ۝ وَلَقَدْ فَتَنَّا ٱلَّذِينَ مِن قَبْلِهِمْ فَلَيَعْلَمَنَّ ٱللَّهُ ٱلَّذِينَ صَدَقُواْ وَلَيَعْلَمَنَّ ٱلْكَٰذِبِينَ ۝ أَمْ حَسِبَ ٱلَّذِينَ يَعْمَلُونَ ٱلسَّيِّـَٔاتِ أَن يَسْبِقُونَا سَآءَ مَا يَحْكُمُونَ ۝

Alif Laam Meem; Do the people think that they will be left to say, "We believe" and they will not be tried? But We certainly tried those before them, and Allah will surely make evident those who are truthful and He will surely make evident the liars. (Soorah Ankaboot; 29: 1-4)

Are there any examples of people who supported the Prophets?

Yes, there are. Amidst all the scorn and ridicule the Prophets faced, there were true believers amongst them, who supported them with vigour.

For example, Eesa, Ibn Maryam alayhe salam (Jesus, the son of Mary) received immediate and unequivocal support from the *al huwairioon* (his disciples). The Qur'aan tells us:

۞ فَلَمَّآ أَحَسَّ عِيسَىٰ مِنْهُمُ ٱلْكُفْرَ قَالَ مَنْ أَنصَارِىٓ إِلَى ٱللَّهِ قَالَ ٱلْحَوَارِيُّونَ نَحْنُ أَنصَارُ ٱللَّهِ ءَامَنَّا بِٱللَّهِ وَٱشْهَدْ بِأَنَّا مُسْلِمُونَ ۝ رَبَّنَآ ءَامَنَّا بِمَآ أَنزَلْتَ وَٱتَّبَعْنَا ٱلرَّسُولَ فَٱكْتُبْنَا مَعَ ٱلشَّٰهِدِينَ

But when Jesus felt [persistence in] disbelief from them, he said: "Who are my supporters for [the cause of] Allah?" Said the Disciples: "We are supporters for Allah. We have believed in Allah and testify that We are Muslims [submitting to Him]. (Soorah Aali 'Imraan; 3:52-53)

And of course we know that Muhammad sallallahu alayhe wasalam was surrounded by sahaabah, companions who supported him in the most phenomenal way. In a famous incident under a tree, a number among the sahaabah, swore an oath of allegiance (*bai'a*) to Muhammad sallallahu alayhe wasalam, an event mentioned in the Qur'aan

۞ لَّقَدْ رَضِىَ ٱللَّهُ عَنِ ٱلْمُؤْمِنِينَ إِذْ يُبَايِعُونَكَ تَحْتَ ٱلشَّجَرَةِ فَعَلِمَ مَا فِى قُلُوبِهِمْ فَأَنزَلَ ٱلسَّكِينَةَ عَلَيْهِمْ وَأَثَٰبَهُمْ فَتْحًا قَرِيبًا ۝

Certainly was Allah pleased with the believers when they pledged allegiance to you [O Muhammad] under the tree, and He knew what was in their hearts and He sent down tranquillity upon them and He rewarded them with an immenent conquest[1]. (Soorah al Fat-h; 48:18)

Were the Prophets human beings like you or I?

Yes. Unlike, you and I, the Prophets were remarkable people with wonderful qualities. However, like you and I, always remember that they were just human beings. Allah tells us of Muhammad sallallahu alayhe wasalam:

$$وَقَالُواْ مَالِ هَٰذَا ٱلرَّسُولِ يَأْكُلُ ٱلطَّعَامَ وَيَمْشِى فِى ٱلْأَسْوَاقِ$$

$$لَوْلَآ أُنزِلَ إِلَيْهِ مَلَكٌ فَيَكُونَ مَعَهُۥ نَذِيرًا ٧$$

And they (the *kuffaar*) say: "What is this messenger that eats food and walks in the markets? Why was there not sent down to him an angel so he would be with him a warner." (Soorah al Furqaan; 25:7)

If they were human beings, how did they perform miracles?

Prophets were given the ability to perform miracles. This was a tool for them to confirm their Prophethood to people around them. For example:

- Musa alayhe salaam, by Allah's leave, changed a stick into a serpent before Pharaoh;
- Esa alayhe salaam, by Allah's leave, moulded clay in his hands into the shape of a bird, blew into it, made it come alive and fly away;
- Muhammad sallallahu alayhe wasalam, by Allah's leave, pointed to the full moon in Makkah, whereupon it split, separated into two half and returned together again.

All these miracles were performed only by the command of Allah. The Prophets were NOT superhuman. They could not perform these miracles as of themselves. Allah reminds us:

$$وَلَقَدْ أَرْسَلْنَا رُسُلًا مِّن قَبْلِكَ وَجَعَلْنَا لَهُمْ أَزْوَٰجًا$$

$$وَذُرِّيَّةً وَمَا كَانَ لِرَسُولٍ أَن يَأْتِىَ بِـَٔايَةٍ إِلَّا بِإِذْنِ ٱللَّهِ لِكُلِّ أَجَلٍ$$

$$كِتَابٌ ٣٨$$

---

[1] the conquest of Khaybar which preceded the conquest of Makkah.

And We have already sent messengers before you and assigned to them wives and descendants: and it was not for a messenger to come with a Sign[1] except by permission of Allah. For every term is a Decree. (Soorah ar Ra'd; 13:38)[2]

Is it obligatory upon all Muslims to believe in the Prophets and Messengers?

Yes. As Muslims, we are required to believe without doubt in all the Prophets of Allah. They were all sent to preach the pure truth of Islaam. Any Muslim who denies any of the Prophets of Allah, falls outside the pale of Islaam and into the realms of *Kufr* (disbelief), may Allah preserve us from that. Allah says:

يَٰٓأَيُّهَا ٱلَّذِينَ ءَامَنُوٓاْ ءَامِنُواْ بِٱللَّهِ وَرَسُولِهِۦ وَٱلْكِتَٰبِ ٱلَّذِى نَزَّلَ عَلَىٰ

رَسُولِهِۦ وَٱلْكِتَٰبِ ٱلَّذِىٓ أَنزَلَ مِن قَبْلُ وَمَن يَكْفُرْ بِٱللَّهِ وَمَلَٰٓئِكَتِهِۦ

وَكُتُبِهِۦ وَرُسُلِهِۦ وَٱلْيَوْمِ ٱلْأَخِرِ فَقَدْ ضَلَّ ضَلَٰلَۢا بَعِيدًا ۝

O you who have believed, believe in Allah and his Messenger and the Book that He has sent down upon His Messenger and the Scripture which He sent down before. And who disbelieves in Allah, His angels, His Books His messengers and the Last Day has certainly gone, far astray. (Soorah an Nisaa'; 4:136)

So, we must believe in ALL the Prophets, not just Muhammad sallallahu alayhe wasalam?

The teachings of the Prophets before Muhammad sallallahu alayhe wasalam have all been superceded by the Qur'aan and the Sunnah. Furthermore, as previously discussed, we know that those teachings have been changed and twisted beyond recognition.

We must believe in all the Prophets without distinction. But we follow only Allah and His Messenger, Muhammad sallallahu alayhe wasalam.

Are all the Prophets the same?

We, as servants of Allah, cannot make any distinctions between the Prophets. The true believer is one, "making no distinction between any of His (Allah's) apostles."[3]

Muhammad sallallahu alayhe wasalam said himself, *"Do not prefer some Prophets to others."*[1]

---

[1] Including miracles
[2] This *ayah* also confirms the human qualities of the Prophets, informing us that they were married with children.
[3] Interpretation of the Meaning of the Qur'aan, Soorah Al Baqarah; 2:285

Having said that, Allah raised some Prophets over others. These were the so called "Messengers of Strong Will". They were, Nuh, Ibraheem, Musa, Esa and Muhammad sallallahu alayhe wasalam.

What was Muhammad sallallahu alayhe wasalam's status amongst them?

To cite Shaikh Muhammad ibn Ibraheem al Tuwayjri: "and the best of the Messengers of Strong Will is Muhammad (peace and blessings of Allaah be upon him). For each Prophet was sent only to his own people, until Allaah sent Muhammad (peace and blessings of Allaah be upon him) to all of mankind. He is the last and the best of the Prophets and Messengers, as Allaah says (interpretation of the meaning) "And We have not sent you (O Muhammad) except as a giver of glad tidings and a warner to all mankind, but most of men know not"[Saba' 34:28 – interpretation of the meaning]"[2]

I suppose the characters of the Prophets were of the highest order?

Yes. They were the very best examples of human kind.

They were the most truthful: *"Also mention in the Book (the story of) Abraham: he was a man of Truth a Prophet. (Interpretation of the Meaning of the Qur'aan - Soorah Maryam; 19:41); And "I am to you an apostle worthy of all trust.[3] (Interpretation of the Meaning of the Qur'aan Soorah Shura'; 26:143)"*

They were patient: *"And (remember) Ismail Idris and Zul-kifl all (men) of constancy and patience;" (Interpretation of the Meaning of the Qur'aan, Soorah Anbiya; 21:85)*

They were often strong and courageous: *"Have patience at what they say and remember Our Servant David the man of strength: for he ever turned (to Allah)." (Interpretation of the Meaning of the Qur'aa,n Soorah Saad; 38:17)*

They were humble: *"For Abraham was without doubt forbearing (of faults) and possessed humility and was and given to look to Allah. (Interpretation of the Meaning of the Qur'aan,* Soorah Hud; 11:75)

They were wise and knowledgeable: *"To Solomon We inspired the (right) understanding of the matter: to each (of them) We gave Judgment and Knowledge; it was Our power that made the hills and the birds celebrate Our praises with David: it was We Who did (these things)." (Interpretation of the Meaning of the Qur'aan, Soorah Anbiya; 21:79)*
Those were just a few examples. Allah says of them generally:

---

[1] Sahih Bukhari; 9:51; narrated by Abu Said
[2] Usool al Deen al Islaami.
[3] Spoken by the Prophet Saleh

$$وَجَعَلْنَـٰهُمْ أَئِمَّةً يَهْدُونَ بِأَمْرِنَا وَأَوْحَيْنَآ إِلَيْهِمْ فِعْلَ ٱلْخَيْرَٰتِ وَإِقَامَ$$

$$ٱلصَّلَوٰةِ وَإِيتَآءَ ٱلزَّكَوٰةِ وَكَانُوا۟ لَنَا عَـٰبِدِينَ ۝$$

And We made them leaders guiding by Our Command and We inspired to them the doing of good deeds, establishment of prayer, and giving zakah, and they were worshippers of Us. (Soorah al Anbiyaa; 21:73)

Wow! So they really were perfect examples for us all?

Yes. In every way. And the most beautiful example of outstanding manners and behaviour can be found in the words and deeds of the Last Prophet Muhammad sallallahu alayhe wasalam. He should be our model to follow and he should be the one that we present to others as the best example of humankind. Allah says,

$$لَّقَدْ كَانَ لَكُمْ فِى رَسُولِ ٱللَّهِ أُسْوَةٌ حَسَنَةٌ لِّمَن كَانَ يَرْجُوا۟ ٱللَّهَ وَٱلْيَوْمَ$$

$$ٱلْأَخِرَ وَذَكَرَ ٱللَّهَ كَثِيرًا ۝$$

There has certainly been for you in the Messenger of Allah an excellent pattern[1] for anyone whose hope is in Allah and the last day, and (who) remembers Allah often. (Soorah al Ahzaab ~ The Combined Forces; 33:21)

I have a friend who loves to read biographies of famous people. He says they give him inspiration? But he has never read any Books about the Prophets.

You will find that many misguided people maintain an active search for comfort and encouragement from the lives of others. They draw their inspiration from all sorts of biographical examples, many of them living, the majority of them dead. They read these works of biography voraciously assisting a multi-billion dollar sub-industry in the world of publishing. Most bookshops in the West are dominated by books about the lives of the late and the "great." Inventors and explorers, presidents and monarchs, sports stars and actors all provide motivational fodder for an all-consuming public.

They read about the way these people struggled and persevered against impossible odds, turning them into super heroes, whilst conveniently ignoring the fact that more often than not, these individuals were hardly the greatest role models.

By the Grace of Allah, we as Muslims are not required to adopt any of these as our role models; in fact they are to be rejected out right. We can refer to the lives of the

---

[1] An example to be followed

truly pious, the Prophets as our guide in life. But our best example should be the life of the Prophet sallallahu alayhe wasalam himself, and his companions. Islaam stands in a pure form today precisely because we are, in the main, following the sunnah. Our behaviour with others, as well as our actual practice of the faith, remains intact because we use Muhammad sallallahu alayhe wasalam as our original reference point. His is the example for use in all our affairs, whether visiting the toilet or undertaking business deals, from dress to devotion.

CHAPTER NINE

Can I ask about Yawm al Aakhir [The Last Day]?

This is the Day after which there will be no more Days. It is the Day when all mankind will be raised to life from the dead, to be judged for their deeds on earth. Every person will be held accountable before Allah for all their deeds.

What do you mean by "held accountable?"

On that Day we will all be made to look back on all the things we did in our lives. We will then either be punished for our bad deeds or rewarded for our good deeds. Those that did bad, will be forced on that Day, to face the evil of what they did. Nobody "gets away" with anything. A person may think that his evil actions are unseen and therefore beyond punishment. On *Yawm al Aakhir* he will realise he was wrong. He will be called to account for ALL his sins, big or small.

Big or small? How small?

The tiniest deeds of man will be judged that Day. Nothing of our deeds on earth has gone unrecorded by the *Malaika* and nothing will pass without judgement on that Day. Allah says:

إِذَا زُلْزِلَتِ ٱلْأَرْضُ زِلْزَالَهَا ۝ وَأَخْرَجَتِ ٱلْأَرْضُ أَثْقَالَهَا ۝ وَقَالَ ٱلْإِنسَـٰنُ مَا لَهَا ۝ يَوْمَئِذٍ تُحَدِّثُ أَخْبَارَهَا ۝ بِأَنَّ رَبَّكَ أَوْحَىٰ لَهَا ۝ يَوْمَئِذٍ يَصْدُرُ ٱلنَّاسُ أَشْتَاتًا لِّيُرَوْاْ أَعْمَـٰلَهُمْ ۝ فَمَن يَعْمَلْ مِثْقَالَ ذَرَّةٍ خَيْرًا يَرَهُۥ ۝ وَمَن يَعْمَلْ مِثْقَالَ ذَرَّةٍ شَرًّا يَرَهُۥ ۝

That Day, the people will depart[1] separated [into categories] to be shown [the result of] their deeds. So whoever does an atom's weight[2] of good will see it, And whoever does an atom's weight of evil will see it. (Soorah Az Zalzaah; 99:6-8)

I have also heard the terms "Day of Ressurection" and "Day of Judgment? Are they referring to the same Day?

The Qur'aan describes Yawm al Aakhir in a number of ways. For example:

1. Yawm-ul-Qiyaamah (The Day of Standing or Day of Ressurection)
2. As-Sa'ah: (The Hour)
3. Yawm-ul-Ba'th, (The Day of Revival from the Dead)
4. Yawm-ul-Khurooj, (The Day of Exit – when all the servants of Allah will exit their graves).
5. Al-Qaari'ah, (The Striking Calamity);
6. Yawm-ul-Fasl, (The Day of Judgment);
7. Yawm-ud-Deen, (The Day of Recompense[3]);
8. Al-Saakhkhah; (Piercing blast of the Horn which signals resurrection);
9. Al-Taamat-ul-Kubra, (The Overwhelming Calamity);
10. Yawm-ul-Hasrah, (The Day of Regret);
11. Al-Ghaashiyyah, (The Overwhelming Event)
12. Yawm-ul-Khulood, (The Day of Eternity);
13. Yawm-ul-Hisaab, (The Day of Accounting – "Allaah will recount/enumerate the actions of the man regarding good and evil, and recount His favours/blessings upon him." – Al Qurtubi);
14. Al-Waaqi'ah, (The Occurrence[4])
15. Yawm-ul-Wa'eed, (The Day of the Threat);
16. Yawm-ul-Aazifah, (The Approaching Day – because it is near);
17. Yawm-ul-Jam'I (The Day of Gathering);
18. Al-Haaqqah, (The Day of the Inevitable Reality);
19. Al-Qiyaamah, (The Day of Resurection);
20. Yawm-ut-Talaaq, (The Day of Meeting);
21. Yawm-ut-Tanaadi, (The Day of Calling[5]);
22. Yawm-ut-Taghaabun, (The Day of Deprivation[6]);
23. Yawm al Hashr, (The Day of Crowding).

---

[1] From the place of Judgement to their final abode. Another interpretation is "emerge separeately" from the graves).

[2] Or the weight of a small ant.

[3] i.e., repayment and compensation for whatever was earned of good or evil during life on this earth.

[4] Literally "that which befalls" meaning the Resurrection.

[5] When the criminals will cry out in terror, the people will call to each other (see 7:44-45), and the angels will call out the results of each person's judgement.

[6] Suggests having been outdone by others in the acquisition of something valued. That Day the disbelievers will suffer the loss of Paradise to the believers.

Is it a must to believe in *Yawm al Aakhir*?

Yes. Denial of the *Yawm al Akhir* places you firmly in *kufr* (disbelief).

$$\text{يَـٰٓأَيُّهَا ٱلَّذِينَ ءَامَنُوٓاْ ءَامِنُواْ بِٱللَّهِ وَرَسُولِهِۦ وَٱلْكِتَـٰبِ ٱلَّذِى نَزَّلَ عَلَىٰ}$$

$$\text{رَسُولِهِۦ وَٱلْكِتَـٰبِ ٱلَّذِىٓ أَنزَلَ مِن قَبْلُۚ وَمَن يَكْفُرْ بِٱللَّهِ وَمَلَـٰٓئِكَتِهِۦ}$$

$$\text{وَكُتُبِهِۦ وَرُسُلِهِۦ وَٱلْيَوْمِ ٱلْأَخِرِ فَقَدْ ضَلَّ ضَلَـٰلًۢا بَعِيدًا ﴿١٣٦﴾}$$

O you who have believed, believe in Allah and his Messenger and the Book that He has sent down upon His Messenger and the Scripture which He sent down before. And who disbelieves in Allah, His angels, His Books His messengers and the Last Day has certainly gone, far astray. (Soorah an Nisaa'; 4:136)

How did the *kuffaar* of Makkah respond when they were threatened with this Day?

They denied it. They mocked the words of the Qur'aan, laughing at the notion that once a person is dead, he will again be raised to life. One day they will see that they were in error and will be severely punished for their mockery. The Qur'aan mentions,

$$\text{ٱلَّذِينَ ٱتَّخَذُواْ دِينَهُمْ لَهْوًا وَلَعِبًا وَغَرَّتْهُمُ ٱلْحَيَوٰةُ ٱلدُّنْيَاۚ}$$

$$\text{فَٱلْيَوْمَ نَنسَـٰهُمْ كَمَا نَسُواْ لِقَآءَ يَوْمِهِمْ هَـٰذَا وَمَا كَانُواْ بِـَٔايَـٰتِنَا}$$

$$\text{يَجْحَدُونَ ﴿٥١﴾}$$

"Who took their religion as distraction and amusement, and whom the worldly life deluded." So today We will forget them just as they forgot the meeting of this day of theirs and for having rejected our verses. (Soorah al A'raaf; 7:51)

$$\text{وَقَالُوٓاْ إِنْ هِىَ إِلَّا حَيَاتُنَا ٱلدُّنْيَا وَمَا نَحْنُ بِمَبْعُوثِينَ ﴿٢٩﴾}$$

And they say: "There is none but our worldly life, and we will not be resurrected." (Soorah al An'aam; 6:29)

I saw a philosophy professor on TV once saying the same thing. He said, once we die, we die! We simply cease to exist! We are just corpses, no more no less.

It seems that despite all his certificates, diplomas and degrees, he doesn't possess that most basic of qualifications, COMMON SENSE! Why doesn't this person reflect upon how he was created in the first place i.e. FROM NOTHING. Allah tells us in the Qur'aan that, as the Supreme Creator, recreating something is no big deal at all.

مِنْهَا خَلَقْنَـٰكُمْ وَفِيهَا نُعِيدُكُمْ وَمِنْهَا نُخْرِجُـكُمْ تَارَةً أُخْرَىٰ ✦

۝

From it [earth] We created you, and into it We will return you, and from it We will extract you another time. (Soorah Ta Ha; 20:55)

The evidence of Allah's power to create, destroy and recreate are all around us, happening every day.

Happening every day? What do you mean?

Yes. Just look at the natural world around you. It is awash with birth, life, death, and rebirth. Destruction and resurrection are routine phenomenan. Green pastures can turn to dustbowls and, with simple H_2O can come to life again. Allah mentions:

وَٱللَّهُ ٱلَّذِىٓ أَرْسَلَ ٱلرِّيَـٰحَ فَتُثِيرُ سَحَابًا فَسُقْنَـٰهُ إِلَىٰ
بَلَدٍ مَّيِّتٍ فَأَحْيَيْنَا بِهِ ٱلْأَرْضَ بَعْدَ مَوْتِهَآ كَذَٰلِكَ ٱلنُّشُورُ ۝

And it is Allah Who sends the Winds, and they stir the clouds, and We drive them to a dead land, and give life thereby to the earth after its lifelessness. Thus is the Resurrection! (Soorah al Faatir; 35:9)

تُولِجُ ٱلَّيْلَ فِى ٱلنَّهَارِ وَتُولِجُ ٱلنَّهَارَ فِى ٱلَّيْلِ وَتُخْرِجُ ٱلْحَىَّ مِنَ ٱلْمَيِّتِ
وَتُخْرِجُ ٱلْمَيِّتَ مِنَ ٱلْحَىِّ وَتَرْزُقُ مَن تَشَآءُ بِغَيْرِ حِسَابٍ ۝

You cause the night to enter the day, and You cause the day to enter the night; and You bring the living out of the dead, and You bring the dead out of the living. And You give provision to whom You will, without account [i.e. limit or measure.]" (Soorah Aali Imraan; 3:27)

$$\text{۞ إِنَّ ٱللَّهَ فَالِقُ ٱلْحَبِّ وَٱلنَّوَىٰ يُخْرِجُ ٱلْحَىَّ مِنَ ٱلْمَيِّتِ وَمُخْرِجُ ٱلْمَيِّتِ}$$
$$\text{مِنَ ٱلْحَىِّ ذَٰلِكُمُ ٱللَّهُ فَأَنَّىٰ تُؤْفَكُونَ ٩٥}$$

Indeed Allah is the cleaver of grain and date seeds, He brings the living out of the dead, and brings the dead out of the living. That is Allah: so how are you deluded? (Soorah al An'aam; 6:95)

What Allah does as a matter of routine in nature, he can do with us with ease on the Day that truly will be the Day of Ressurection.

Yes. Allah is Almighty. He can do anything.

Yes. Anyone who thinks otherwise or seeks to limit His Powers is arrogant and has placed himself in *kufr* (disbelief).

$$\text{أَيَحْسَبُ ٱلْإِنسَٰنُ أَلَّن نَّجْمَعَ عِظَامَهُ ٣}$$

Does man think that We will not assemble his bones? (Soorah al Qiyaamah; 75:3)

Is Judgement Day a metaphorical day or is it real?

The Day of Judgement is an awesome Day. There is no doubt about its reality or its coming.

$$\text{فَكَيْفَ إِذَا جَمَعْنَٰهُمْ لِيَوْمٍ لَّا رَيْبَ فِيهِ وَوُفِّيَتْ}$$
$$\text{كُلُّ نَفْسٍ مَّا كَسَبَتْ وَهُمْ لَا يُظْلَمُونَ ٢٥}$$

So how will it be when We assemble them for a Day about which there is no doubt? And each soul will be compensated [in full for] what it earned, and they will not be wronged. (Soorah Aali Imraan; 3:25)

Yawm Al Aakhir is *Haq.*[1] It is a promise that will be fulfilled. It is a Day upon which, all those who denied and disagreed over it, will come to realise that it is fact and not fiction. At one stage in the Qur'aan, Allah repeats this point saying (Interpretation of the Meaning of), "Verily they will come to know; Again verily they will come to know."(Soorah an Nabaa; 78:4-5)

---

[1] The Truth, an inevitable reality

The good people are those who believe in it without doubt and hold the meeting with Allah on that Day firmly in their hearts.

$$ٱلَّذِينَ يَظُنُّونَ أَنَّهُم مُّلَـٰقُوا۟ رَبِّهِمْ وَأَنَّهُمْ إِلَيْهِ رَٰجِعُونَ ۝$$

Who are certain that they will meet their Lord, and that they will return to Him. (Soorah al Baqarah; 2:46)

So they live their lives fearful of that Day?

Yes. Every step they take, every action they perform, every utterance from their lips, in fact in all aspects of their lives they live in the knowledge that they will face a Mighty Judgement on a Fiercesome Day.

What about the disbelievers

The evil ones are those who are satisfied with the life of this world and take no heed of the fact that they will be raised again to stand before Allah Subhaan wa Ta'aala. Allah says,

$$إِنَّ ٱلَّذِينَ لَا يَرْجُونَ لِقَآءَنَا وَرَضُوا۟ بِٱلْحَيَوٰةِ ٱلدُّنْيَا وَٱطْمَأَنُّوا۟$$
$$بِهَا وَٱلَّذِينَ هُمْ عَنْ ءَايَـٰتِنَا غَـٰفِلُونَ ۝$$

Indeed, those who do not expect the meeting with Us, and are satisfied with the life of this world and feel secure therein, and those who are heedless of Our Signs. (Soorah Yoonus; 10:7)

When will *Yawm al Aakhir* take place?

Only Allah Subhaana knows the timing of this Day.

$$يَسْـَٔلُكَ ٱلنَّاسُ عَنِ ٱلسَّاعَةِ قُلْ إِنَّمَا عِلْمُهَا عِندَ ٱللَّهِ وَمَا يُدْرِيكَ$$
$$لَعَلَّ ٱلسَّاعَةَ تَكُونُ قَرِيبًا ۝$$

People ask you concerning the Hour. Say, "Knowledge of it is only with Allah. And what may make you perceive? Perhaps the Hour is near!" (Soorah al Azhaab; 33:63)

Is it's time fixed already?

Yes, it is fixed and, as Allah says (interpretation of the meaning), "We do not delay it except for a limited term[1]" To cite Ibn Kathir[2], "It is an actual day only Allah knows but it is fixed, its appointment can neither be delayed nor brought forward"

Will anyone be available to help us that Day?

That Day will be very severe for those who did wrong on earth. There will be no one on that Day to help the sinners. Brothers cannot help brother, friends cannot help friends: The Qur'aan mentions,

$$ ٱلۡأَخِلَّآءُ يَوۡمَئِذٍۭ بَعۡضُهُمۡ لِبَعۡضٍ عَدُوٌّ إِلَّا ٱلۡمُتَّقِينَ ۝ $$

Close friends that Day will be enemies to each other; except for the Righteous. (Soorah az Zukraf; 43:67)[3]

Even your own kith and kin, whom you loved so much on earth, will be too preoccupied with saving themselves on that Mighty Day, as described in the Qur'aan,

$$ يَوۡمَ يَفِرُّ ٱلۡمَرۡءُ مِنۡ أَخِيهِ ۝ وَأُمِّهِۦ وَأَبِيهِ ۝ وَصَٰحِبَتِهِۦ وَبَنِيهِ ۝ لِكُلِّ ٱمۡرِيٕٖ مِّنۡهُمۡ يَوۡمَئِذٍ شَأۡنٌ يُغۡنِيهِ ۝ $$

On the Day a man will flee from his brother And his mother and his father, And his wife and his children. For every man, that Day, will be a matter adequate for them[4]. (Soorah 'Abasa; 80:34-37)

Even your own parents will forsake you? How can that be?

We are informed that it will be. Your parents had compassion and mercy for you whilst you were on earth, but on that Day, they will only think of themselves.

Even mothers, people who are normally revered on earth for their mercy towards their own children, will abandon that mercy and their children, just to save themselves. Allah Ta'aala tells us,

---

[1] Soorah al Hood; 11:104

[2] From his tafseer.

[3] "On that Day shall no intercession avail except for those for whom permission has been granted by (Allah) Most Gracious and whose word is acceptable to Him." (interpretation of the meaning of Soorah Taha; 20:109)

[4] i.e. to occupy him. He will be concerned only with himself, thus forgetting all others.

94

$$\text{يَوْمَ تَرَوْنَهَا تَذْهَلُ كُلُّ مُرْضِعَةٍ عَمَّا أَرْضَعَتْ وَتَضَعُ كُلُّ ذَاتِ حَمْلٍ}$$

$$\text{حَمْلَهَا وَتَرَى ٱلنَّاسَ سُكَٰرَىٰ وَمَا هُم بِسُكَٰرَىٰ وَلَٰكِنَّ عَذَابَ ٱللَّهِ شَدِيدٌ}$$

On the Day you see it, every nursing mother will be distracted from that [child] she was nursing, and every pregnant woman will abort her pregnancy, and you will see the people [appearing] intoxicated while they are not intoxicated; but the punishment of Allah is severe. (Soorah Al Hajj; 22:2)

Just stop and think how frightening that Day will be, if even your own mother gives you up. That Day will be a Day of rank selfishness and terror, with all around ONLY thinking of THEMSELVES.

How will the arrival of Yawm al Aakhira be announced?

By the blowing, twice, of a pearcing trumpet. The Qur'aan states,

$$\text{وَنُفِخَ فِى ٱلصُّورِ فَصَعِقَ مَن فِى ٱلسَّمَٰوَٰتِ وَمَن فِى ٱلْأَرْضِ إِلَّا}$$

$$\text{مَن شَآءَ ٱللَّهُ ثُمَّ نُفِخَ فِيهِ أُخْرَىٰ فَإِذَا هُم قِيَامٌ يَنظُرُونَ}$$

And the Horn will be blown and whoever is in the heavens and whoever is on earth will fall dead except as Allah wills. Then it will be blown again, and at once they will be standing, looking on. (Soorah az Zumar; 39:68)

Also

$$\text{يَوْمَ يُنفَخُ فِى ٱلصُّورِ فَتَأْتُونَ أَفْوَاجًا}$$

The Day the Horn is blown and you will come forth in multitudes. (Soorah an Naba'; 78:18)

In the last Ayah, it mentions people coming in "multitudes." What does that mean?

The ancient scholar At Tabari[1] states that it means every community will come forth with its messengers.

---

[1] Also quoted by Ibn Katheer in his tafseer

So for every nation from the past or present, a Prophet will come forward?

Allah tells us,

$$يَوْمَ نَدْعُواْ كُلَّ أُنَاسٍ بِإِمَـٰمِهِمْ$$

> [Mention, O Mohammed], the Day we will call forth every people with their record of deeds (or "with the leader" or "with that which they had followed") (Soorah al Israa' 17: 71)

That's a lot of people! Are you saying that anyone who has ever existed will be raised to life?

Yes, everyone. All the past generations will raise from their graves and stand up again for their judgement. They will rise from the earth like vegetables growing from the ground.

> Abu Hurairah narrates that the Messenger of Allah sallallahu alayhe was sallam said "between the two blows [of the trumpet], is forty." They asked, "Forty days?" He replied, "I refuse (to answer)" "They asked: Forty years?" He said, "I refuse". Then he said, "Then Allah will send down from the heavens water causing mankind to grow like vegetables (from the earth). Nothing remains of the man except the coccyx (tail bone) and from it mankind will be (re-)created on the Day of Resurrection.

Will *malaika* be present also?

Yes, although they face no Judgement, they will be present that Day, also in multitudes. The Qur'aan states, (interpretation of the meaning), "And the Heaven is open and becomes as gates" (Soorah an Nabaa'; 78:19). Ibn Katheer states in his tafseer, "That is, it will become a way of descent for the angels."

What about animals, will they also be gathered?

Yes[1].

$$وَمَا مِن دَآبَّةٍ فِى ٱلْأَرْضِ وَلَا طَـٰٓئِرٍ يَطِيرُ بِجَنَاحَيْهِ إِلَّآ أُمَمٌ أَمْثَالُكُم مَّا$$
$$فَرَّطْنَا فِى ٱلْكِتَـٰبِ مِن شَىْءٍ ثُمَّ إِلَىٰ رَبِّهِمْ يُحْشَرُونَ ۝$$

> And there is no creature on [or within] the earth or bird that flies with its wings, except [that they are] communities like you. We have not neglected in the

---

[1] Although a number of commentators including Ibn Kathir state that this gathering of beasts will be for their death only, ultimately leaving only mankind and jinn behind.

Register[1] a thing. Then unto their Lord they will be gathered gathered. Surah 6:38.

Also in the Surah Taqveer, Yawm al Aakhir is described as the Day (interpretation of the meaning), "when the wild beasts are hearded together[2]"

Will the earth be destroyed?

It will be a Day of total destruction. In fact, the earth will be levelled flat. The Qur'aan tells us,

$$\text{وَيَسْـَٔلُونَكَ عَنِ الْجِبَالِ فَقُلْ يَنسِفُهَا رَبِّى نَسْفًا ۞ فَيَذَرُهَا قَاعًا صَفْصَفًا ۞ لَّا تَرَىٰ فِيهَا عِوَجًا وَلَآ أَمْتًا ۞}$$

And they ask you about the mountains, so say, "Lord will blow them away with a blast." And he we will leave it [i.e. the earth] a level plain. You will not see therein a depression or elevation. (Soorah Ta Ha; 20:105-107)

How can mountains be blown away?

Just picture that. Can you think of anything more firm or steadier than a mountain. Trees are firm but they will eventually fall down or they can be chopped down. Buildings are firm but they too can collapse. Mountains have the strongest image. However, on Yaum al Qayaamah they, (interpretation of the meanings), "will float away like clouds[3]" and "become like cotton balls[4]".

Is Yawm al Qiyaamah near?

Yes. It is nearer than you think. So take heed. Don't spend your life procrastinating about good deeds, "I will be good tomorrow Insha Allah, I will change my ways Insha Allah!" No! Do it now. You don't know when you will die and as Allah reminds us, (interpretation of the meaning), "verily we warn a doom at hand." (Soorah Nabah 78:40)

---

[1] The Preserved Tablet (al Lawh al Mahfoodh), in which all things are recorded.
[2] 81:5
[3] 27:88
[4] 101:5

The State of the kuffaar on Yawm al Aakhir as mentioned in the Qur'aan

They will ask for respite –

وَأَنذِرِ ٱلنَّاسَ يَوْمَ يَأْتِيهِمُ ٱلْعَذَابُ فَيَقُولُ ٱلَّذِينَ ظَلَمُوا۟ رَبَّنَآ أَخِّرْنَآ إِلَىٰٓ

أَجَلٍ قَرِيبٍ نُّجِبْ دَعْوَتَكَ وَنَتَّبِعِ ٱلرُّسُلَّ أَوَلَمْ تَكُونُوٓا۟ أَقْسَمْتُم مِّن قَبْلُ

مَا لَكُم مِّن زَوَالٍ ۝

And, [O Muhammad], warn the people of a Day when the punishment will come to them and those who did wrong-will say: "Our Lord, delay us for a short term,; we will answer Your Call, and follow the Messengers!" {But it will be said], "Had you not sworn, before, that for you there would be no cessation? (Soorah al Ibraheem; 14:44)

They will be blind –

وَمَنْ أَعْرَضَ عَن ذِكْرِى فَإِنَّ لَهُۥ مَعِيشَةً ضَنكًا وَنَحْشُرُهُۥ

يَوْمَ ٱلْقِيَٰمَةِ أَعْمَىٰ ۝ قَالَ رَبِّ لِمَ حَشَرْتَنِىٓ أَعْمَىٰ وَقَدْ كُنتُ

بَصِيرًا ۝ قَالَ كَذَٰلِكَ أَتَتْكَ ءَايَٰتُنَا فَنَسِيتَهَا وَكَذَٰلِكَ ٱلْيَوْمَ

تُنسَىٰ ۝

And whoever turns away from my rememberance – indeed he will have a depressed [i.e. difficult] life, and We will gather [i.e. raise] him on the Day of Resurrection blind. He will say, "My Lord. Why have you raised me blind while I was [once] seeing?" [Allah] will say, "Thus did Our signs come to you, and you forgot, [i.e. disregarded] them; and thus will you this Day be forgotten." (Soorah Ta Ha; 20:124-126)

They will ask to be sent back to earth –

فَمَا لَنَا مِن شَـٰفِعِينَ ۝ وَلَا صَدِيقٍ حَمِيمٍ ۝ فَلَوْ أَنَّ لَنَا
كَرَّةً فَنَكُونَ مِنَ ٱلْمُؤْمِنِينَ ۝

"So now we have no intercessors and not a devoted friend. Then if we only had a return [to the world] and could be of the believers...."[1] (Soorah ash Shu'araa'; 26:100-102)

They will wrangle with and blame each other –

وَقَالَ ٱلَّذِينَ كَفَرُوا لَن نُّؤْمِنَ بِهَـٰذَا ٱلْقُرْءَانِ وَلَا بِٱلَّذِى بَيْنَ يَدَيْهِ وَلَوْ
تَرَىٰ إِذِ ٱلظَّـٰلِمُونَ مَوْقُوفُونَ عِندَ رَبِّهِمْ يَرْجِعُ بَعْضُهُمْ إِلَىٰ بَعْضٍ ٱلْقَوْلَ
يَقُولُ ٱلَّذِينَ ٱسْتُضْعِفُوا لِلَّذِينَ ٱسْتَكْبَرُوا لَوْلَا أَنتُمْ لَكُنَّا مُؤْمِنِينَ

۝

And those who disbelieve say: "We will never believe in this Qur'aan, nor in that before it." But if you could see when the wrongdoers are made to stand before their Lord, refuting each others' words....[2] Those who were oppressed will say to those who were arrogant, "If not for you, we would have been believers!" (Soorah Saba'; 34:31)

No ransom will be accepted from them

إِنَّ ٱلَّذِينَ كَفَرُوا وَمَاتُوا وَهُمْ كُفَّارٌ فَلَن يُقْبَلَ مِنْ أَحَدِهِم مِّلْءُ
ٱلْأَرْضِ ذَهَبًا وَلَوِ ٱفْتَدَىٰ بِهِ أُوْلَـٰئِكَ لَهُمْ عَذَابٌ أَلِيمٌ وَمَا لَهُم مِّن
 نَّـٰصِرِينَ ۝

---

[1] The conclusion of this verse is estimated as "…..we would do this or that."
[2] Having been left to the imagination, the conclusion of this sentence is estimated to be "….you would see a dreadful sight."

Indeed those who disbelieved and die while they are disbelievers – never would the [whole] capacity of earth in gold be accepted from one of them if he would [seek to] ransom himself with it. For those there will be a painful punishment, and they will have no helpers.(Soorah Aali Imraan; 3:91)

The idols of idolators will reject them –

كَلَّا سَيَكْفُرُونَ بِعِبَادَتِهِمْ وَيَكُونُونَ عَلَيْهِمْ ضِدًّا ﴿٨٢﴾

No! They [i.e. those "gods" they worshipped] will deny their worship of them and will be against them opponents [on the Day of Judgment]. (Soorah Maryam; 19:82)

They will be confronted with their evil –

فَلَنَقُصَّنَّ عَلَيْهِم بِعِلْمٍ وَمَا كُنَّا غَآئِبِينَ ﴿٧﴾

Then We will surely relate [their deeds] to them with knowledge, and We were not [at all] absent. (Soorah al A'raaf; 7:7)

Their body parts will testify against them –

يَوْمَ تَشْهَدُ عَلَيْهِمْ أَلْسِنَتُهُمْ وَأَيْدِيهِمْ وَأَرْجُلُهُم بِمَا كَانُواْ يَعْمَلُونَ ﴿٢٤﴾

On the Day when their tongues, their hands, and their feet will bear witness against them as to what they used to do. (Soorah Noor; 24:24)

And as for the good:

ٱنظُرْ كَيْفَ فَضَّلْنَا بَعْضَهُمْ عَلَىٰ بَعْضٍ وَلَلْآخِرَةُ أَكْبَرُ دَرَجَٰتٍ وَأَكْبَرُ تَفْضِيلًا ﴿٢١﴾

[Mention, O Mohammed], the Day we will call forth every people with their record of deeds Then whoever is given his record in his right hand, those will read their records and injustice will not be done to them, [even] as much as a thread [inside a date seed]. (Soorah al Israa' 17: 71)

يَـٰٓأَيُّهَا ٱلَّذِينَ ءَامَنُوا۟ تُوبُوٓا۟ إِلَى ٱللَّهِ تَوْبَةً نَّصُوحًا عَسَىٰ رَبُّكُمْ أَن يُكَفِّرَ

عَنكُمْ سَيِّـَٔاتِكُمْ وَيُدْخِلَكُمْ جَنَّـٰتٍ تَجْرِى مِن تَحْتِهَا ٱلْأَنْهَـٰرُ

يَوْمَ لَا يُخْزِى ٱللَّهُ ٱلنَّبِىَّ وَٱلَّذِينَ ءَامَنُوا۟ مَعَهُۥ ۖ نُورُهُمْ يَسْعَىٰ

بَيْنَ أَيْدِيهِمْ وَبِأَيْمَـٰنِهِمْ يَقُولُونَ رَبَّنَآ أَتْمِمْ لَنَا نُورَنَا وَٱغْفِرْ لَنَآ ۖ إِنَّكَ

عَلَىٰ كُلِّ شَىْءٍ قَدِيرٌ ﴿٨﴾

O you who have believed, repent to Allah with sincere repentance. Perhaps[1]
your Lord will remove from you your misdeeds and admit you into Gardens
beneath which rivers flow [on] the Day Day when Allah will not disgrace the
Prophet and those who believed with him. Their Light will proceed before them
and on their right, they will say, "Our Lord! Perfect for us our Light, and forgive
us. Indeed You are over all things competent." (Soorah ath Tahreem; 66:8)

يَوْمَ نَحْشُرُ ٱلْمُتَّقِينَ إِلَى ٱلرَّحْمَـٰنِ وَفْدًا ﴿٨٥﴾

On the Day We will gather the righteous to The Most Merciful as a delegation.
(Soorah Maryam; 19:85)

لَا يَحْزُنُهُمُ ٱلْفَزَعُ ٱلْأَكْبَرُ وَتَتَلَقَّىٰهُمُ ٱلْمَلَـٰٓئِكَةُ هَـٰذَا يَوْمُكُمُ ٱلَّذِى كُنتُمْ

تُوعَدُونَ ﴿١٠٣﴾

They will not be grieved by The Greatest Terror, and the angels will meet them
[saying] "This is your Day, which you have been promised." Soorah al Anbiyaa'
21:103)

---

[1] Emigrating for the Cause of Allah

CHAPTER TEN

Can I ask about Al Jahannam and wal Jannah [Hell and Paradise]?

Jahannam is commonly known in English as "Hell." It is a dreadful place. It is a place of indescribable torment. A place of incredible, humiliation, pain and suffering. It is a permanent home made ready for those who broke Allah's commandments, rejected His Messengers or did not believe in Him altogether.

Jannah is commonly known in English as "Heaven" or "Paradise." It is a fantastic place. Whatever superlative adjectives are used, still they cannot describe *Jannah*. It is the home of those who lived their lives on earth in obedience to Allah, for those who remained constantly aware of His presence, living in fear of His punishment and in Hope of His Mercy. It is the ultimate reward for their good deeds.

Do we go to *Jahannam* or *Jannah* directly after we die?

No, these places will only start to be inhabited after the Day of Judgment. We will be judged first on that Day, and then either punished with *Jahannam* or rewarded with *Jannah*.

So where will we remain from the moment of death until the *Yawm al Qiyaamah*?

In our graves. Our graves will not be the physical places you see when the earth is dug. As our interim abode until Judgment Day, they will be transformed. If we were bad in our lives, they will become places of anguish and torment. If we were *saleh*, (righteous) they will be like Gardens of Paradise.

Where are these places located? Is *Jahanam* in the center of the earth? Is *Jannah* above the clouds?

There is no reliable evidence of the location of *Jahannam* or *Jannah* either in the Qur'aan or the sahih Sunnah. Consequently we do not know where they are and neither should we speculate. The consensus amongst the *ulema* is that this Knowledge is with Allah alone.

Have *Jahannam* and *Jannah* already been created, although they are empty?

Yes, they have. This is the opinion, based on informed sources, of the reliable scholars of the past. To quote one of them, Sheikh Tahhaawi, "Paradise and Hell have already been created. They will never come to end or cease to exist. Allah created Paradise and Hell before the rest of creation and He created inhabitants for each of them."

This view is contrary to some misguided sects in the past, who held that Allah will create *Jahannam* and *Jannah* only on *Yawm al Qiyaamah*[1]. The Qur'aan and ahadith clearly demonstrate that this notion is false.

In the Qur'aan (interpretation of the meaning),

$$\text{وَٱتَّقُواْ ٱلنَّارَ ٱلَّتِىٓ أُعِدَّتْ لِلْكَـٰفِرِينَ ۝}$$

And fear the Fire, which has been prepared for the disbelievers. (Soorah Aali Imraan; 3:131)

$$\text{سَابِقُوٓاْ إِلَىٰ مَغْفِرَةٍ مِّن رَّبِّكُمْ وَجَنَّةٍ عَرْضُهَا كَعَرْضِ ٱلسَّمَآءِ وَٱلْأَرْضِ}$$
$$\text{أُعِدَّتْ لِلَّذِينَ ءَامَنُواْ بِٱللَّهِ وَرُسُلِهِۦ ۚ ذَٰلِكَ فَضْلُ ٱللَّهِ يُؤْتِيهِ مَن يَشَآءُ ۚ}$$
$$\text{وَٱللَّهُ ذُو ٱلْفَضْلِ ٱلْعَظِيمِ ۝}$$

Race [i.e. compete] toward forgiveness from your Lord, and a Garden whose width is like the width of the heavens and the earth, prepared for those who believed in Allah and His messengers. That is the Bounty of Allah, which He gives to whom He wills, Allah is the Possessor of Great Bounty. (Soorah al Hadeed; 57:21)

From the ahadith

Abdullah ibn Umar narrates that Muhammad sallallahu alayhe wasallam said, "When anyone of you dies, he will be shown his

---

[1] The Mu'tazilah, Qaadiriyah and Jahamiyyah sects said this.

position morning and evening. If he is one of the people of Paradise, then he will be one of the people of Paradise, and if he is one of the people of Hell, then he will be one of the people of Hell, and he will be told: "this is your position, until Allah resurrects you on the Day of Resurrection." (Reported in Bukhari and Muslim)

Also Muslim reports from Anas that the Prophet sallallahu alayhe wasallam said, "By the One in Whose hand is my soul, if you had seen what I saw, you would laugh little and cry much." They said, "What did you see, O Messenger (sallallahu alayhe wasallam)" He said, "I saw Paradise and Hell."

How will people enter *Jahannam* ?

Through seven gates. These gates are layered one above the other. They will be crammed full with sinners. Once the inhabitants have entered, the gates will be locked shut behind them. None will be able to escape. Allah warns us (interpretation of the meaning):

$$ وَإِنَّ جَهَنَّمَ لَمَوْعِدُهُمْ أَجْمَعِينَ ۞ لَهَا سَبْعَةُ أَبْوَابٍ لِّكُلِّ بَابٍ مِّنْهُمْ $$

$$ جُزْءٌ مَّقْسُومٌ ۞ $$

And indeed, Hell is the promised place for them all! It has seven gates: for every gate is of them a portion designated (i.e. a special class of sinners assigned for every gate). (Soorah Al Hajj; 15:43-44)

And *Jannah*?

Through eight gates. The righteous will enter through particular gates in accordance with their good deeds. For example, those who fasted, will enter through a gate called *rayaan*.

Sahl Ibn Sa'd said that Muhammad sallallahu alayhe wasallam said, "There are eight gates to Paradise. One of them is a gate called *Al Rayyaan* and none shall enter it excet those who observe fasting." (Al Bukhari)

Who will be there to greet the inhabitants of *Jahannam* as they enter?

Angels will receive them with cynical words of scorn. The Qur'aan says (interpretation of the meaning),

وَسِيقَ ٱلَّذِينَ كَفَرُوٓاْ إِلَىٰ جَهَنَّمَ زُمَرًا ۖ حَتَّىٰٓ إِذَا جَآءُوهَا فُتِحَتْ أَبْوَٰبُهَا

وَقَالَ لَهُمْ خَزَنَتُهَآ أَلَمْ يَأْتِكُمْ رُسُلٌ مِّنكُمْ يَتْلُونَ عَلَيْكُمْ ءَايَٰتِ

رَبِّكُمْ وَيُنذِرُونَكُمْ لِقَآءَ يَوْمِكُمْ هَٰذَا ۚ قَالُواْ بَلَىٰ وَلَٰكِنْ حَقَّتْ كَلِمَةُ

ٱلْعَذَابِ عَلَى ٱلْكَٰفِرِينَ ۝ قِيلَ ٱدْخُلُوٓاْ أَبْوَٰبَ جَهَنَّمَ خَٰلِدِينَ

فِيهَا ۖ فَبِئْسَ مَثْوَى ٱلْمُتَكَبِّرِينَ ۝

And those who disbelieved will be driven to Hell in groups until when they reach it, its gates are opened and its keepers will say, "Did there not come to you messengers from yourselves, reciting to you the verses of your Lord, and warning you of the Meeting of this Day of yours?" They will say, "Yes, but the Decree of Punishment has come into effect upon the disbelievers." [To them] it will be said, "Enter the gates of Hell to abide eternally therein, and wretched is the residence of the arrogant."(Soorah az Zumar; 39;71-72)

There are nineteen angels guarding *Jahannam* (Qur'aan – 74:30). By Allah's command they are harsh and stern towards the people of *Jahannam*.

And what of the reception for the people of *Jannah*?

Angels will receive them with the most beautiful words imaginable as mentioned in the Qur'aan (interpretation of the meanings),

وَسِيقَ ٱلَّذِينَ ٱتَّقَوْاْ رَبَّهُمْ

إِلَى ٱلْجَنَّةِ زُمَرًا ۖ حَتَّىٰٓ إِذَا جَآءُوهَا وَفُتِحَتْ أَبْوَٰبُهَا وَقَالَ لَهُمْ خَزَنَتُهَا

But those who feared their Lord will be driven to Paradise in groups until, when they reach it while its gates have been opened and its keepers say, "Peace be upon you; you have become pure; so enter it to abide eternally therein,"(Soorah az Zumar; 39:73)

ٱدْخُلُوهَا بِسَلَٰمٍ ۖ ذَٰلِكَ يَوْمُ ٱلْخُلُودِ ۝

"Enter it in peace, This is the Day of Eternity. (Soorah all Qaf; 50:34)

How big is *Jahannam*?

Gigantic. Consider just two factors:

1. If you dropped a huge rock into Jahamman, it would take seventy years to reach the bottom[1].

2. It will be filled with every sinner that has ever walked the earth. Interpretation of the meaning of the Qur'aan:

$$لَأَمْلَأَنَّ جَهَنَّمَ مِنكَ وَمِمَّن تَبِعَكَ مِنْهُمْ أَجْمَعِينَ ۝$$

"That I will surely fill Hell with you and those of them that follow you all together." (Soorah Saad; 38:85)

But, furthermore, each of those sinners will be gigantic.

Abu Hurayrah narrates that Muhammad sallallahu alayhe wasallam said, "The distance between the shoulders of the kaafir in Hell will be like three days' travelling for a fast rider." (Muslim)[2]

And what about the size of *Jannah*?

This place is gigantic also. If I tell you how gigantic the gates alone of *Jannah* are, that will give you an idea about the size of *Jannah* itself.

Utbah ibn Ghazwaan narrates, "We are told that the distance between the gate panels of one of the gates of Paradise is like the distance of forty years walking, but there will come a time when it is very crowded indeed." (Reported in Muslim and Ahmed)

What if, out of two evil doers, one is more evil than the other? Are their punishments in *Jahannam* the same?

Jahannam has many levels. The Qur'aan inform us, (interpretation of the meaning),

---

[1] Hakim reports from Abu Hurayrah, (and Tabaraani from Mu'adh and Abu Ummamah) that the Prophet sallallahu alayhe wasallam said, "If there was a huge stone as big as seven *khalfaat* stones, and it was thrown from the edge of Hell, it would fly through it for seventy years before it reached the bottom." Sahih al Jaami' as Sagheer, 5/58, no. 5124 with sahih isnaad.

[2] According to An Nawawee, "all of this is in order to intensify the suffering and all of this is possible for Allah". (Sharh al Nawawee 'alaa Muslim 17/186).

So is one who pursues the pleasure of Allah like one who brings upon himself the anger of Allah, and whose refuge is Hell? And wretched is the destination. They are [varying] degrees in the sight of Allah, and Allah is seeing of whatever they do. (Soorah Aali Imraan; 3:162-163)

The lowest level of *Jahannam* is reserved for the munafiqeen (the hypocrites). Allah tells us, (interpretation of the meaning),

إِنَّ ٱلۡمُنَٰفِقِينَ فِى ٱلدَّرۡكِ ٱلۡأَسۡفَلِ مِنَ ٱلنَّارِ وَلَن تَجِدَ لَهُمۡ نَصِيرًا ۝

Indeed the hypocrites will be in the lowest depths of the Fire; and never will you find for them a helper. (Soorah an Nisaa';4:145)

Are there different levels to Paradise also?

This is only fair. If you spent all your working hard for a *Jannah* that is invisible to you to please your Lord whom you also cannot see, then InshAllah, you can expect tremendous rewards. Allah tells us, (interpretation of the meaning),

ٱنظُرۡ كَيۡفَ فَضَّلۡنَا بَعۡضَهُمۡ عَلَىٰ بَعۡضٖۚ وَلَلۡأٓخِرَةُ أَكۡبَرُ دَرَجَٰتٖ وَأَكۡبَرُ تَفۡضِيلًا ۝

Look how we have favoured [in provision] some of you over others. But the Hereafter is greater in degrees [of difference] and greater in distinction. (Soorah al Israa; 17:21)

Bukhari reports from Abu Hurayrah radhiAllaho anho that the Prophet sallallahu alayhe was sallam said, "Whoever believes in Allah and His Messenger sallallahu alayhe was sallam, offers prayer perfectly and fasts in the month of Ramadhaan, will be granted Paradise as a right by Allah, no matter whether he fights in Allah's cause or remains in the land where he was born." The people said:, "O Messenger of Allah (sallallahu alayhe was sallam), shall we acquaint the people with this good news?" He sallallahu alayhe was sallam said, "Paradise has one hundred levels which Allah has reserved for the *Mujahiddeen* who fight in His cause, and the distance between each of the two grades is like the distance between the heavens and the earth. So when you ask Allah for something, ask for *al Firdaws* which is the best and highest part of Paradise. I (narrator) think he said, "Above it (*Al Firdaws*) is the Throne of the Most Merciful, and from it originate the rivers of Paradise[1]."

How long do *Jahannam* and *Jannah* last?

Neither will ever cease to exist. They will both last forever. This is the opinion of the reliable scholars of our *ummah*. To cite Sheikh Ibn Taymiyyah, "The *Salaf* (first generation) and *imams* (leaders) of this *ummah*, and the *Ahl As Sunnah Wa al Jammah*, agreed that there are created entities that will never come to an end at all, like Paradise, Hell, The Throne and so on[2]."

If those places exist forever, will their inhabitants remain there forever? Will people stay in *Jahannam* forever?

The following categories of people will remain in *Jahannam* forever:

1. *Kuffaar* (disbelievers);
2. *Mushrikeen* (idolators);
3. Those who followed other systems and beliefs of the *kuffaar* over the *shari'ah* of Allah;[3]
4. *Munaafiqeen* (hypocrites);
5. The Arrogant.

Allah tells us about the above (interpretation of the meanings),

وَٱلَّذِينَ كَذَّبُواْ بِـَٔايَـٰتِنَا وَٱسۡتَكۡبَرُواْ عَنۡهَآ أُوْلَـٰٓئِكَ أَصۡحَـٰبُ ٱلنَّارِۖ

هُمۡ فِيهَا خَـٰلِدُونَ ٣٦

But the ones who deny our verses and are arrogant toward them – those are the Companions of the Fire, They will abide therein eternally.(Soorah al A'raaf; 7:36)

إِنَّكُمۡ وَمَا تَعۡبُدُونَ مِن دُونِ ٱللَّهِ حَصَبُ جَهَنَّمَ أَنتُمۡ لَهَا وَٰرِدُونَ ٩٨

Indeed, you [disbelievers] and what you worship other than Allah, are the firewood fuel for Hell! You will be coming to [enter] it. (Soorah al Anbiyaa; 21:98)

---

[1] The highest position in Paradise is *Al Waseela*. InshaAllah that will be attained by one person only, Muhammad sallallahu alayhe was sallam.
[2] Majmaa' fataawaa 18/307
[3] e.g. socialism, capitalism, communism, constitutional democracy etc.

يَوْمَ تُقَلَّبُ وُجُوهُهُمْ فِى ٱلنَّارِ يَقُولُونَ يَلَيْتَنَآ أَطَعْنَا ٱللَّهَ وَأَطَعْنَا

ٱلرَّسُولَا ۝ وَقَالُواْ رَبَّنَآ إِنَّآ أَطَعْنَا سَادَتَنَا وَكُبَرَآءَنَا فَأَضَلُّونَا ٱلسَّبِيلَاْ

The Day their faces will be turned about in the Fire, they will say: "How we wished we had obeyed Allah and obeyed the Messenger!" And they will say, "Our Lord! Indeed we obeyed our masters and our dignitaries, and they led us astray from the [right] path." (Soorah al Azhaab; 33:66-67)

In the Qur'aan *Jahannam* is described as an "abode" for the disbelievers, i.e. a permanent home as opposed to a temporary halting point.

Do the people of *Jannah* also live there forever?

All those that enter Paradise remain there forever. Allah tells us (interpretation of the meaning),

إِنَّ ٱلَّذِينَ ءَامَنُواْ وَعَمِلُواْ ٱلصَّلِحَاتِ كَانَتْ لَهُمْ جَنَّاتُ ٱلْفِرْدَوْسِ نُزُلًا

خَلِدِينَ فِيهَا لَا يَبْغُونَ عَنْهَا حِوَلًا ۝

Indeed those who have believed and done righteous deeds, they will have the Gardens of Paradise, as a lodging, Wherein they abide eternally. They will not desire from it any transfer.(Soorah al Khaf; 18:107-108)

The inhabitants of Paradise will never be forced to leave it, and neither will they die. They will experience its pleasures for all eternity.

Abu Hurayrah radhiAllaho anho narrates that Muhammad sallallahu alayhe was sallam said, "Whoever enters Paradise is blessed with a life of joy; he will never feel miserable, his clothes will never wear out and his youth will never fade away." (Sahih Muslim)

All inhabitants of Paradise will be a youthful thirty-three years old. Ahmed and Tirmidhi report from Mu'aadh ibn Jabal that the Messenger of Allah sallallahu alayhe was sallam said, "The people of Paradise will enter Paradise hairless, looking as if their eyes are ringed with kohl, aged thirty-three.

What happens to those kuffaar who did good in their lives? And what about those adherents to Islaam and tawheed, who did evil?

If He wills, Allah will reward all *kuffaar* for their good deeds. However that reward will be in the world only, the world which they love and crave so much. They will be deprived of the rewards of the *aakhira* because all the good they did was surrounded by the most heinous sins of *kufr* and *shirk*.

Eventually, all those who, in the main, submitted to the Will of Allah and avoided associating partners with Him, will be sent to *Jannah*. Whilst *Jahannam* is the "abode" for the above mentioned categories of sinners, *Jahannam* will be the place of "temporary" torment for those who accepted Islaam and tawheed but committed punishable sins. Those people will enter *Jahannam* for a period known only to Allah, but will thereafter be admitted to Paradise.

Do the people of *Jahannam* eat?

Yes, including the following food:

1. *Ad Dari*; - Ibn Abbaas says that Ad Dari is "a low growing thorny plant." Qartadah said, "it is one of the very worst types of food."[1]
2. *Az Zaqqoom*; - We are informed in the Qur'aan about this food, interpretation of the meanings, "Is that the better entertainment or the Tree of Zaqqum? For We have truly made it (as) a trial for the wrong-doers. For it is a tree that springs out of the bottom of Hell-fire: The shoots of its fruit-stalks are like the heads of devils: Truly they will eat thereof and fill their bellies therewith. Then on top of that they will be given a mixture made of boiling water. Then shall their return be to the (Blazing) Fire." (Soorah as Saaffat; 37:62-68)
3. *Al Ghaslin*; - This is the filth that eminates for example after washing wounds. (69:35-37);
4. *An Naar*; Fire (4:10 and 2:174)

What food do the people of *Jannah* eat?

Insha'Allah anything our hearts desire will be available in *Jannah*. It will be food, delicious to taste and without all the consequences that we face on earth (bloating, weight gain, excretion etc). The Qur'aan mentions fruit and foul specifically, (interpretation of the meanings), "In both of them are of every fruit, two kinds." (Soorah ar Rahmaan; 55:52), and "And fruit of what they select."(Soorah al Waaqi'ah; 56:20)

---

[1] Ibn Rajab, *Al takhweef min al naar*, quoted by Sheikh Al Ashqar in *Al Jannah wan Naar*

What will the people of these places drink?

In Jahannam,

1. *Al Hameem* – Boiling water. The Qur'aan tells us of this in numerous places e.g. (interpretation of the meaning), "They will be relieved with water like murky oil which scalds their faces. Wretched is the drink and evil is the resting place." (18:29)
2. *Al Ghassaaq* – A disgusting pus like fluid that oozes from the bodies of the people of Hell themselves. Although it is so vile, those very people will thirst for this drink.
3. *As Sadeed* – Pus
4. *Al Muhl* – Boiling Oil. Abu Sa'eed al Khudri narrates as reported by Ahmed and Tirmidhi, that the Prophet sallallahu alayhe was sallam said, "It is like boiling oil, and when it is bought near a person's face, the skin of the face falls off into it.[1]"

What will people drink in *Jannah*?

Wine! Yes, wine! This will be just one of the drinks available there. It will be a wine free of the side effects, complications and ill consequences associated with wine on earth. It will be pure to taste and will not dull the senses.

There will circulate among them young boys made eternal with vessels, pitchers and a cup [of wine] from a flowing spring – No headache will they have therefrom, nor will they be intoxicated. (Soorah al Waaqi'ah; 56:17-19)

What will the people of *Jahannam* wear? Is it possible to wear anything in the fire?

Their clothes themselves will be fire as Allah tells us, (interpretation of the meaning), "But those who disbelieved will have cut out for them garments of fire." (Soorah al Hajj; 22:19).

Also, (interpretation of the meaning), "And you will see the criminals that Day bound together in shackles, their garments of liquid pitch and their faces covered by fire. (Soorah Ibraheem; 14;49:50)"

And what will the people of *Jannah* wear?

وَجَزَىٰهُم بِمَا صَبَرُواْ جَنَّةً وَحَرِيرًا ﴿١٢﴾

---

[1] Ibn Abbaas commented that "it is like very thick oil."

And will reward them for what they patiently endured [with] a garden [in Paradise] and silk [garments]. (Soorah al Insaan;76:12)

إِنَّ ٱللَّهَ يُدْخِلُ ٱلَّذِينَ ءَامَنُوا۟ وَعَمِلُوا۟ ٱلصَّٰلِحَٰتِ جَنَّٰتٍ تَجْرِى مِن تَحْتِهَا ٱلْأَنْهَٰرُ يُحَلَّوْنَ فِيهَا مِنْ أَسَاوِرَ مِن ذَهَبٍ وَلُؤْلُؤًا ۖ وَلِبَاسُهُمْ فِيهَا حَرِيرٌ ۝

Indeed, Allah will admit those who believe and do righteous deeds to gardens beneath which rivers flow. They will be adorned therein with bracelets of gold and pearl, and their garments therein will be silk. (Soorah al Hajj; 22:23)

Scorching of faces

يَوْمَ تُقَلَّبُ وُجُوهُهُمْ فِى ٱلنَّارِ يَقُولُونَ يَٰلَيْتَنَآ أَطَعْنَا ٱللَّهَ وَأَطَعْنَا
ٱلرَّسُولَا ﴿٦٦﴾

The Day their faces will be turned about in the Fire, they will say, "How we wish we had obeyed Allah and obeyed the Messenger." (Soorah al Ahzaab; 33:66)

Fire all around

لَهُم مِّن جَهَنَّمَ مِهَادٌ وَمِن فَوْقِهِمْ غَوَاشٍ وَكَذَٰلِكَ نَجْزِى ٱلظَّٰلِمِينَ ﴿٤١﴾

They will have from Hell a bed and over them coverings [of fire]. And thus do We recompense the wrongdoers. (Soorah al A'raaf; 7-41)

Tied with chains and fetters

إِذِ ٱلْأَغْلَٰلُ فِىٓ أَعْنَٰقِهِمْ وَٱلسَّلَٰسِلُ يُسْحَبُونَ ﴿٧١﴾

When the shackles are around their necks and the chains; they will be dragged [in boiling water] (Soorah Ghaafir;40:71)

seized by hooks of iron

وَلَهُم مَّقَٰمِعُ مِنْ حَدِيدٍ ﴿٢١﴾ كُلَّمَآ أَرَادُوٓاْ أَن يَخْرُجُواْ مِنْهَا مِنْ
غَمٍّ أُعِيدُواْ فِيهَا وَذُوقُواْ عَذَابَ ٱلْحَرِيقِ ﴿٢٢﴾

And for [striking] them are maces of iron. Everytime they want to get out of it [i.e. Hellfire] from anguish, they will be returned to it, and [it will be said], "Taste the punishment of the Burning Fire!" (Soorah al Hajj; 22:- 21-22)

No evil talk

$$\text{لَّا يَسْمَعُونَ فِيهَا لَغْوًا وَلَا كِذَّابًا ﴿٣٥﴾}$$

No ill speech will they hear therein or any falsehood (Soorah an Naba';78:35)

With servants

$$\text{يَطُوفُ عَلَيْهِمْ وِلْدَانٌ مُّخَلَّدُونَ ﴿١٧﴾ بِأَكْوَابٍ وَأَبَارِيقَ وَكَأْسٍ مِّن مَّعِينٍ ﴿١٨﴾}$$

There will circulate among them young boys made eternal with vessels, pitchers and a cup [of wine] from a flowing spring – (Soorah al Waaqi'ah; 56:17-18)

They will be with friends

$$\text{وَنَزَعْنَا مَا فِى صُدُورِهِم مِّنْ غِلٍّ إِخْوَانًا عَلَىٰ سُرُرٍ مُّتَقَابِلِينَ ﴿٤٧﴾}$$

And we will remove whatever is in their breasts of resentments, [so they will be] brothers, on thrones facing each other. (Soorah al Hijr; 15:47)

The most beautiful wives

$$\text{إِنَّ لِلْمُتَّقِينَ مَفَازًا ﴿٣١﴾ حَدَائِقَ وَأَعْنَابًا ﴿٣٢﴾ وَكَوَاعِبَ أَتْرَابًا ﴿٣٣﴾ وَكَأْسًا دِهَاقًا ﴿٣٤﴾}$$

Indeed for the righteous is attainment, Gardens and grapevines and full breasted [companians] of equal age. (Soorah an Naba'; 78:31-33)

CHAPTER ELEVEN

Can I ask about Al Qadar [Preordination]?

Qadar is variously translated using such words as "Destiny", "Fate" or "Preordination." Basically it is the reality that everything that occurs in Allah's universe was already decreed to occur by Him. The subject of Qadar is also often called Al Qada wal Qadar (Divine Decree and Preordination).

Everything?

Yes, EVERYTHING, big or small, open or hidden, good or bad, EVERYTHING. Everything in His creation happens according to His exact Will. Everything occurs by His Power according to His exact measure. The Scholar of Islaam, Sheikh Ibn Taymiyyah identified four aspects to belief in Qadar[1]. They are:
1.   Belief in the Prior Knowledge of Allah;
2.   Belief in the Writing of the Book of Decrees;
3.   Belief in the Ultimate Power and Will of Allah;
4.   Belief in the Creation of Everything by Allah.

Please explain each of those?

1.   Belief in the Prior Knowledge of Allah;

This is the absolute belief by a Muslim that Allah has prior knowledge of everything. He knows what is manifest and open as well as that which is hidden deep in the hearts.

---

[1] As defined in his work, *Shahr Al Aqeedat Al Wasitiyah.*

He knew beforehand everything that would happen to His creation, whether by His own Will or through the Will of His creation.

To quote Ibn Taymiyyah, "It is the belief that Almighty Allah knew what His creations were going to do through His prior knowledge which is perpetually associated with Him. He knew all their circumstances of obedience and disobedience, of their allotment and their death."

Allah mentions in the Qur'aan:

$$\text{۞ وَمَا مِن دَآبَّةٍ فِى ٱلْأَرْضِ إِلَّا عَلَى ٱللَّهِ رِزْقُهَا وَيَعْلَمُ مُسْتَقَرَّهَا وَمُسْتَوْدَعَهَا كُلٌّ فِى كِتَٰبٍ مُّبِينٍ ﴿٦﴾}$$

And there is no creature on earth but that upon Allah is its provision, And He knows its place of dwelling and place of storage[1]. All is in a clear register. (Soorah Hood; 11:6)

$$\text{ٱللَّهُ يَعْلَمُ مَا تَحْمِلُ كُلُّ أُنثَىٰ وَمَا تَغِيضُ ٱلْأَرْحَامُ وَمَا تَزْدَادُ وَكُلُّ شَىْءٍ عِندَهُۥ بِمِقْدَارٍ ﴿٨﴾}$$

Allah knows what every female carries[2] and what the wombs lose [prematurely] or exceed[3]. And everything with Him is by due measure.(Soorah al Raad; 13:8)

$$\text{۞ وَعِندَهُۥ مَفَاتِحُ ٱلْغَيْبِ لَا يَعْلَمُهَآ إِلَّا هُوَ وَيَعْلَمُ مَا فِى ٱلْبَرِّ وَٱلْبَحْرِ وَمَا تَسْقُطُ مِن وَرَقَةٍ إِلَّا يَعْلَمُهَا وَلَا حَبَّةٍ فِى ظُلُمَٰتِ ٱلْأَرْضِ وَلَا رَطْبٍ وَلَا يَابِسٍ إِلَّا فِى كِتَٰبٍ مُّبِينٍ ﴿٥٩﴾}$$

With Him are the keys of the Unseen, the treasures that none knoweth but He. He knoweth whatever there is on the earth and in the sea. Not a leaf doth fall but with His knowledge: there is not a grain in the darkness (or depths) of the

---

[1] Before birth and after death.
[2] With absolute knowledge inclusive of every aspect of the fetus' existence.
[3] Beyond their normal period of pregnancy ans/or the number of fetuses therein.

117

earth, nor anything fresh or dry (green or withered), but is (inscribed) in a Record clear (to those who can read). (Soorah al An'aam; 6:59)

2.   Belief in the Book of Decrees;

This is the absolute belief by a Muslim that Allah had written everything that was to happen in a special Book.

So everything that happens to me on earth, good or bad, or everything I do, good or evil was written down beforehand?

Yes. The destiny of all Allah's creation was written down beforehand. Allah says in the Qur'aan:

أَلَمْ تَعْلَمْ أَنَّ ٱللَّهَ يَعْلَمُ مَا فِى ٱلسَّمَآءِ وَٱلْأَرْضِ إِنَّ ذَٰلِكَ فِى كِتَٰبٍ إِنَّ ذَٰلِكَ عَلَى ٱللَّهِ يَسِيرٌ ٧٠

Do you not know that Allah knows what is in the heaven and earth? Indeed, that is in a record. Indeed that for Allah is easy. (Soorah al Hajj; 22:70)

مَآ أَصَابَ مِن مُّصِيبَةٍ فِى ٱلْأَرْضِ وَلَا فِىٓ أَنفُسِكُمْ إِلَّا فِى كِتَٰبٍ مِّن قَبْلِ أَن نَّبْرَأَهَآ إِنَّ ذَٰلِكَ عَلَى ٱللَّهِ يَسِيرٌ ٢٢

No disaster strikes upon the earth or among yourselves except that it is in a register before we bring it into being – indeed that, for Allah, is easy – (Soorah al Hadeed; 57:22)

What is the name of this Book?

It is called *Al Lauh Al Mahfoodh* (The Safe Tablet). In fact, according to one hadith, the Pen, (*Al Qalam*) that was used to write this Book, was one of the first things that Allah created.

> The first thing that Allah created was the Pen. He asked it to write and the pen asked what should it write about. Allah asked him to write out whatever is determined to take place up until the Day of Resurrection. (Abu Dawood - Al *Qadar*, mentioned by Ibn Taymiyyah)[1].

3.   Belief in the Ultimate Power and Will of Allah;

This is the absolute belief by a Muslim in the Ultimate Power and Will of Allah. He tells us:

$$\text{لِمَن شَآءَ مِنكُمْ أَن يَسْتَقِيمَ ۝ وَمَا تَشَآءُونَ إِلَّا أَن يَشَآءَ ٱللَّهُ رَبُّ ٱلْعَٰلَمِينَ ۝}$$

For whoever wills among you to take a right course. And you do not will except that Allah wills – Lord of the worlds. (Soorah ath Takweer; 81:28-29)

$$\text{هُوَ ٱلَّذِى يُصَوِّرُكُمْ فِى ٱلْأَرْحَامِ كَيْفَ يَشَآءُ لَآ إِلَٰهَ إِلَّا هُوَ ٱلْعَزِيزُ ٱلْحَكِيمُ ۝}$$

It is He Who forms you in the wombs however He Wills. There is no deity except Him, the Exalted in Might, the Wise.(Soorah Aali Imraan; 3:6)

$$\text{وَلَوْ شَآءَ رَبُّكَ لَآمَنَ مَن فِى ٱلْأَرْضِ كُلُّهُمْ جَمِيعًا أَفَأَنتَ تُكْرِهُ ٱلنَّاسَ حَتَّىٰ يَكُونُوا۟ مُؤْمِنِينَ ۝ وَمَا كَانَ لِنَفْسٍ أَن تُؤْمِنَ إِلَّا بِإِذْنِ ٱللَّهِ وَيَجْعَلُ ٱلرِّجْسَ عَلَى ٱلَّذِينَ لَا يَعْقِلُونَ ۝}$$

---

[1] There is a difference of opinion amongst the ulema as to which was created first, Al Arsh (The Throne), or Al Qalam (The Pen).

And had your Lord Willed, those on earth would have believed – all of them entirely. Then [O, Muhammad], would you compel the people in order that they may become believers? And it is not for a soul [i.e. anyone] to believe, except by permission of Allah, and He will place defilement[1], upon those who will not use reason. (Soorah Yoonus; 10:99-100)

So we as Muslims believe that His Will is the Supreme Will.

Yes. Nothing, nothing can exist without His Will. Nothing can happen without His Will. His Will is total and all encompassing. To quote Ibn Taymiyyah, it is to believe that "whatever Allah Wills is going to be and whatever He does not wish, will never take place. It is to believe that no motion or stillness in heaven or earth can occur without the Almighty's Will. There can be nothing in His Kingdom that He does not intend to be."

4. Belief in the creation of everything by Allah from nothing;

This is the absolute belief by a Muslim that Allah created everything.

This appears to be Tawheed Al Rubuiyyah?

Yes, it is connected to that. There is nothing, be it inanimate or living, that was not created by Allah. He is the creator of everything and, indeed, the only creator of everything.

$$وَٱللَّهُ خَلَقَكُمْ وَمَا تَعْمَلُونَ ﴿٩٦﴾$$

"While Allah created you and that which you do" (Soorah al Saffaat; 37:96)

$$ٱلَّذِى خَلَقَ ٱلْمَوْتَ وَٱلْحَيَوٰةَ لِيَبْلُوَكُمْ أَيُّكُمْ أَحْسَنُ عَمَلًا وَهُوَ ٱلْعَزِيزُ ٱلْغَفُورُ ﴿٢﴾$$

[He] Who created Death and Life, to test you [as to] which of you is best in deed; and He is the Exalted in Might, the Forgiving; (Soorah al Mulk; 67:2)

$$هُوَ ٱلَّذِى خَلَقَكُم مِّن طِينٍ ثُمَّ قَضَىٰٓ أَجَلًا وَأَجَلٌ مُّسَمًّى عِندَهُۥ ثُمَّ أَنتُمْ تَمْتَرُونَ ﴿٢﴾$$

---

[1] Among its meanings are filth, punishment, disbelief, confusion and error.

It is He ho created you from clay, and then decreed a term[1] and a specified time [known] to Him[2]; yet you are in dispute. (Soorah al An'aam; 6:2)

Is it a must to believe in *Qadar*?

Yes. Absolutely. Belief in Al *Qadar* is one of the arkaan al eemaan, (Pillars of Faith). You cannot claim to believe in the other parts of faith, but then decide not to believe in Al *Qadar*.

Al *Qadar* is part of Al ghaib (the unseen). Even though the knowledge of *Qadar* is with Allah, we must still believe that it exists. If we do not, we fall outside Islaam and into kufr (disbelief).

Does the belief in *Qadar* mean that man has no Power or Will of his own to do anything?

This view was a held by the sold called *Al Jabariyah*, a misguided sect in the past. They asserted that we are all simply "victims" of fate, helpless and powerless, unable to determine anything in our lives.

The consensus of the sensible and correct opinion is that this is wrong.

So then, to use a well-worn expression in the Non Muslim world, are we the "Masters of our own Destiny?"

This is the other extreme of the position mentioned in your previous question, and was asserted by another deviant sect, Al Qaadiriyah. This belief states that humans are totally in control of everything in relation to their destiny. Such opinion holds that they alone, without Allah's involvement, have the power and the complete freedom of choice to determine the outcome of their own affairs.

This is another dangerous and false notion. Allah can never be kept out of anything in relation to His creation.

So then where does man's will stand in the concept of *Qadar*? What is the correct position regarding man's will?

Basically, man has power, will and freedom of choice. However, this power, will and freedom of choice is:
1. an aspect of his creation, granted by Allah;
2. limited in its nature.

---

[1] An appointed time for death.
[2] For resurrection.

So Allah has given man, power and will, but only in some things and not in others?

Yes.

What kinds of things are beyond the will of man?

The weather for example is beyond man's control. The weather can act in way which may easily inconvenience your life, but you would remain powerless to do anything about it.

I left home yesterday on foot, and it started to rain. I got wet.

Without a good umbrella, your getting wet was inevitable. That rainfall and you getting wet was something beyond your control.

Your example is a petty one. More seriously, the weather has the propensity to change people's lives altogether.

For example?

Consider the farmer who, because of heavy rainfall and flooding, loses his entire harvest for the year, or the fisherman's wife whose husband's boat fails to return from stormy seas.

- Both these situations were decreed beforehand;
- Both these situations resulted in personal ruin and suffering.
- Both these situations were beyond their control.

Earthquakes are another example that come to mind. Man has no control over the movements of the earth.

Yes. An earthquake could be part of a person's *Qadar*. It is something he has no control over, yet it has the potential to destroy his life.

The same applies to disease, pestilence and life and death itself.

$$\text{أَيْنَمَا تَكُونُوا يُدْرِككُّمُ الْمَوْتُ وَلَوْ كُنتُمْ فِى بُرُوجٍ مُّشَيَّدَةٍ}$$

"Wherever you may be, death will overtake you, even if you should be in towers of lofty construction. (Soorah an Nisaa'; 4:78)

There are aspects of are own body too that are beyond our power and will. Tell me can you control the way your left ventricle moves inside your heart?

122

Left ventricle? I don't know where it is let alone control it!

Can you control how much fluid your kidneys will process today, or how your blood will flow through your veins in the next ten minutes?

No obviously, I can't. I have no control over those actions in my own body.

These events and thousands more like them, take place every second in your body without you intending them and outside of your control. So whether we are discussing rain fall, or seizmic movements of the earth or the functioning of our own bodies, you can see there are so many factors that are beyond our control, factors that demonstrate clearly that man is NOT the "master of his own destiny."

Tell me about those actions within our control.

You cannot stop it raining, as mentioned before, but you can minimise the degree to which you will get wet, by leaving home with a good umbrella. It is within your will whether you decide to take an umbrella.

So we have the ability to choose in limited situations.

Yes. Consider the example of our bodies again. You may not be able to control your heart movements or your kidney functioning. However, you can choose by yourself what your eyes will see. You can decide of your own accord, what your hands will do, what your toungue will say and where your legs will take you. You can also decide yourself, what your private parts will get up to.

We have been given the ability by Allah to choose for ourselves, whether those organs remain engaged in good or evil.

This is a return to the subject of "Free Will?"

Yes, free will, as discussed in our chapter about *Al Malaika*. Remember, unlike **malaika**, we have the ability to choose whether to do good or bad. We, as humans, can choose either to follow *siraat al mustaqeem* (the straight path) or to follow the path of wrongdoing and sin.

We will be held accountable for those things that lie within our choice. The eminent Sheikh Uthaimeen rahmatullah alay gives a good example when he states, "The person who reaches safely the bottom of a flight of stairs knows that this is because he walked down carefully. However, if he is pushed down from the top, he has no power over how he lands at the bottom. The first instance is an example of choice, the second is clearly one of compulsion."

It makes sense therefore that if man does evil, he can be punished for that evil, because he has chosen to do it. In this limited sense, he is the master of his own destiny.

It is only right that such a person should be punished for the evil things he has control over and which he has chosen to do.

- Nobody forces evildoers to lie, cheat or steal; They do it because they want to.
- Nobody forces evildoers to commit zina. They only does so because they refuse to fear Allah;
- Nobody forces evildoers not to perform salah. They arrogantly "choose" to disobey Allah;
- Nobody forces an evildoer to secretly eat in Ramadhan. No hand will come out of the fridge and grab them by the throat!

All these people have complete freedom to behave however they like. However, they should know that there are consequences for all their evil actions, consequences that they bought upon themselves.

Similarly, will Allah reward those righteous people who choose to follow his commands?

Yes. Its good that you used the word "choose." Saleh people "choose" to do good and for that, InshAllah they will be rewarded.

You mentioned that part of faith in *Qadar* is belief that Allah has prior knowledge of everything? Does that include prior knowledge as to whether a person will do good or sin?

Allah knows everything. He has prior knowledge of all the actions of His creation. He knows what lies in our future and what lay in our past.

If it is written in a person's *Qadar* already that he will do evil, why should Allah punish him at all?

As mentioned Allah knows everything about His creation. That includes knowing beforehand the choices his creation will make. Just because Allah knows someone will make bad choices and commit evil, that doesn't mean that the punishment for making that bad choice should be lessened.

Imagine that you are planning to cheat in your school exams. Imagine that your teacher has found out from another source what you have in mind. Imagine, that, even though he knows beforehand you are going to cheat, he still lets go ahead and commit the act. When you get caught, are you going to protest that you shouldn't be punished because your teacher knew about what you were planning? Regardless of what your teacher knew, you made the bad choice yourself and you should be punished.

It scares me to think that I may have evil actions already written in my *Qadar*.

Don't be preoccupied with what may or may not be in your *Qadar*. The matter and knowledge of *Qadar* lies with Allah alone.

Just think about your actions day to day. Try your best to maximise your good deeds and eliminate your bad deeds so that you can please Allah and achieve *Jannah*. Remember, you have the complete free will to do that.

I often hear it mentioned that Allah guides whom He wills and sends astray whom he will?

Allah says:

$$\text{مَن يَهْدِ ٱللَّهُ فَهُوَ ٱلْمُهْتَدِى ۖ وَمَن يُضْلِلْ فَأُوْلَٰئِكَ هُمُ ٱلْخَٰسِرُونَ} \quad ﴾١٧٨﴿$$

Whoever Allah guides, - he is the [rightly] guided; and whoever He sends astray[1] – it is those who are losers. (Soorah al A'raaf; 7:178)

$$\text{مَن يُضْلِلِ ٱللَّهُ فَلَا هَادِىَ لَهُۥ ۚ وَيَذَرُهُمْ فِى طُغْيَٰنِهِمْ يَعْمَهُونَ}$$
$$﴾١٨٦﴿$$

Whoever Allah sends astray - there is no guide for Him. And He leaves them in their transgression, wandering blindly. (Soorah al A'raaf; 7:186)

If a person has already been "sent astray" by Allah, how can that person then be punished?

Remember. Allah is not inequitable. He will NEVER punish a person unjustly. He only punishes those people who bring punishment upon themselves. Similarly, he will only send astray those who, by their words and deeds, demonstrate that they want to be sent astray. They bring Allah's lack of Guidance upon themselves.

How can they bring "lack of guidance" upon themselves?

If their hearts are not inclined towards Islam in the first place, Allah will let them continue blindly upon the path of error.

---

[1] As a result of persistence in evil and rejection of truth.

If their hearts are inclined to gross disobedience to Allah, in the first place, Allah may well seal their hearts altogether.

Shouldn't Allah's Guidance be available to all?

Allah's Guidance (*Hidayah*) will not be available to those who, despite all the signs, arrogantly choose to deny Him, and persist in that denial.

$$\text{إِنَّ ٱلَّذِينَ كَفَرُوا سَوَآءٌ عَلَيْهِمْ ءَأَنذَرْتَهُمْ أَمْ لَمْ تُنذِرْهُمْ}$$

$$\text{لَا يُؤْمِنُونَ ۝ خَتَمَ ٱللَّهُ عَلَىٰ قُلُوبِهِمْ وَعَلَىٰ سَمْعِهِمْ وَعَلَىٰٓ}$$

$$\text{أَبْصَٰرِهِمْ غِشَٰوَةٌ وَلَهُمْ عَذَابٌ عَظِيمٌ ۝}$$

Indeed, those who disbelieve, it is all the same for them whether you warn them or do not warn them; they will not believe. Allah has set a seal upon their hearts and upon their hearing, and over their vision is a veil; And for them is a great punishment. (Soorah al Baqarah; 2:6-7)

Notice above that before Allah talks about setting the seal, He has mentions that they are the ones who reject faith. They are the ones who made the first serious mistake of *kufr*. Allah only confounds them further.

If Allah cuts His guidance to kuffaar, how is it that some among them end up embracing Islam?

For those who show even the slightest inclination towards Islam, Tawheed and obedience to Allah, if He Wills, He will smooth their path towards Islam. He says:

$$\text{فَمَن يُرِدِ ٱللَّهُ أَن يَهْدِيَهُ يَشْرَحْ صَدْرَهُ لِلْإِسْلَٰمِ وَمَن يُرِدْ أَن يُضِلَّهُ}$$

$$\text{يَجْعَلْ صَدْرَهُ ضَيِّقًا حَرَجًا كَأَنَّمَا يَصَّعَّدُ فِى ٱلسَّمَآءِ كَذَٰلِكَ يَجْعَلُ}$$

$$\text{ٱللَّهُ ٱلرِّجْسَ عَلَى ٱلَّذِينَ لَا يُؤْمِنُونَ ۝}$$

So whoever Allah wants to guide, He expands his breast to [contain] Islam; And whoever He wants to misguide, He makes his breast tight and constricted, as though he were climbing into the sky. Thus does Allah place defilement upon those who do not believe. (Soorah al An'aam; 6:125)

Such *kaafir* only embrace Islaam, because who gives them *hidayah*.

Even the stubborn and hard-hearted ones?

Only Allah knows the state of someone's heart. A *kaafir* may appear on the surface stubborn, incalcitrant and rude, whilst harbouring a desire for the truth in some deep, distant light filled corner of their heart. As long as that desire and light is there, if He wills, Allah will give them hidayah.

If it is possible that a *kaafir*, through Allah's guidance can be guided towards Islam, is it possible that a Muslim, through His lack of Guidance, could be guided towards *Kufr*?

This is a frightening but entirely real possibility. Just because many of us were born Muslim, we should never take this gift for granted. We should always seek to strengthen our *eemaan*, always be weary of the tricks of shaytaan, and always prayer to Allah that He lets us die as Muslims. He mentions a *du'a* in the Qur'aan:

رَبَّنَا لَا تُزِغْ قُلُوبَنَا بَعْدَ إِذْ هَدَيْتَنَا وَهَبْ لَنَا مِن لَّدُنكَ رَحْمَةً إِنَّكَ أَنتَ الْوَهَّابُ ۝ رَبَّنَا إِنَّكَ جَامِعُ النَّاسِ لِيَوْمٍ لَّا رَيْبَ فِيهِ إِنَّ اللَّهَ لَا يُخْلِفُ الْمِيعَادَ ۝

[Who say] Our Lord! Let not our hearts deviate after You have guided us and grant us from Yourself mercy. Indeed, you are the Bestower.

"Our Lord! Surely You will gather the people for a Day about which there is no doubt. Indeed Allah does not fail in His promise. (Soorah Aali Imraan; 3:8-9)[1]

Is my livelihood already decreed?

Your livelihood (*rizq*) has been preordained. How much you will earn, where and when you will earn it, are all matters fixed already by Allah. He says:

---

[1] This du'a is worth remembering. Transliterated it is:
RABB ANNA - LAA TUZIGH QULOOBANAA
BA'DA 'IDH HADAYTA -NAA
WA- HAB LA- -NAA MIL LADUN -KA RAHMAH
'INNA -KA 'ANTA AL- WAHHAAB;
RABB -NAA 'INNA -KA JAAMI' AN- NAAS
LI- YAWM LAA RAYB FE -HI
'INNA 'ALLAAH LAA YUKHLIF AL- ME' AAD

إِنَّ ٱللَّهَ عِندَهُۥ عِلْمُ ٱلسَّاعَةِ وَيُنَزِّلُ ٱلْغَيْثَ وَيَعْلَمُ مَا فِى ٱلْأَرْحَامِ وَمَا تَدْرِى نَفْسٌ مَّاذَا تَكْسِبُ غَدًا وَمَا تَدْرِى نَفْسٌ بِأَيِّ أَرْضٍ تَمُوتُ إِنَّ ٱللَّهَ عَلِيمٌ خَبِيرٌ ۝

Indeed, Alllah [alone] has knowledge of the Hour and sends down the rains and knows what is in the wombs[1]. And no soul perceives what it will earn tomorrow, and no soull perceives in what land it will die. Indeed, Allah is Knowing and Acquainted. (Soorah Luqmaan; 31:34)

If my *rizq* has been preordained, why should I be to concerned about it? Is it still necessary for me to work hard at my studies and eventually in my chosen profession?

- A general leading an army of *mujahideen*, cannot tell his men to put down their weapons simply because he believes, whether they win or lose, it is *Qadar*Allah anyway – they must struggle, as the *sahaabah* did to uphold Islam on the earth;
- A student of Islamic knowledge cannot simply sit at home with his books closed waiting for knowledge to enter his brain – He must struggle to acquire the knowledge that has been decreed for him;
- A chicken shawarma maybe in your *rizq* for lunch today – but you still have to drive to the restarant, pay the money and eat it.

How can *Qadar* help me in my life?

Real *eemaan* comes from understanding completely that everything in our lives good or bad has been preordained by Allah. Understanding this makes us feel grateful to Allah for what he has given us (as opposed to having pride in ourselves). It prevents us from feeling sorrow or regret for what He, in His Almighty Wisdom, has not given us. Allah tells us:

مَآ أَصَابَ مِن مُّصِيبَةٍ فِى ٱلْأَرْضِ وَلَا فِى أَنفُسِكُمْ إِلَّا فِى كِتَٰبٍ مِّن قَبْلِ أَن نَّبْرَأَهَآ إِنَّ ذَٰلِكَ عَلَى ٱللَّهِ يَسِيرٌ ۝ لِّكَيْلَا تَأْسَوْا۟ عَلَىٰ مَا فَاتَكُمْ وَلَا تَفْرَحُوا۟ بِمَآ ءَاتَىٰكُمْ وَٱللَّهُ لَا يُحِبُّ كُلَّ مُخْتَالٍ فَخُورٍ ۝

---

[1] i.e. every aspect of the fetus' present and future existence.

No misfortune can happen on earth or in your souls but is recorded in a decree before We bring it into existence: that is truly easy for Allah. In order that ye may not despair over matters that pass you by, nor exult over favours bestowed upon you. For Allah loveth not any vainglorious boaster (Soorah al Hadeed; 57;22:23)

Al Qadar

Consider the following examples. What would your attitude be in these circumstances?

Story One

You are the manager in a large company. You learn that someone is talking behind your back and aggressively by word and deed against you. He may well be trying to unseat you and get your job.

- **I will carry on doing the job to the very best of my ability regardless of events around me;**
- **Of course, I will not be silly and close my eyes to what is happening – I will be cautious of him, but not overly suspicious, because be overly suspicious could be a sin in itself;**
- **I will try my best and then have faith in Allah.**

Yes. You should know that no one can harm you or help you in life, other than Allah – NO ONE. If this man wanted to d something to you, he couldn't unless it was decreed by Allah Almighty Himself.

This example mentions only one man. Even if all the nations of the world were out to get you, they could not do so unless the matter was decreed by Allah.

Allah's Messenger sallallahu alayhe wasallam said to Ibn Abbas radhiAllaho anho, "Know that if the whole community collaborated to benefit you, they would not benefit you except through what is preordained by Allah. And if they collaborated to harm you with something, they would not inflict harm except what is preordained. Pens and papers are dried. (Sahih Muslim).

And we are told in the Qur'aan:

قُل لَّن يُصِيبَنَآ إِلَّا مَا كَتَبَ ٱللَّهُ لَنَا هُوَ مَوْلَىٰنَا وَعَلَى ٱللَّهِ فَلْيَتَوَكَّلِ

ٱلْمُؤْمِنُونَ ۝

Say: "Never will we be struck except by what Allah has decreed for us; He is our Protector": and upon Allah let the Believers rely. (Soorah at Tawbah; 9:51)

Story Two

An earthquake hits your city. You lose members of your family, your home and all your possessions.

- I will have *sabr* (patience) because *sabr* is always rewarded by Allah especially in severe circumstances, like the one you have mentioned.
- I will accept that whatever bad has happened to me was ordained by the One in whose Hands is my entire life, Allah, the Most High.
- I will agree to whatever He has agreed for me;
- I will slowly try to rebuild my life, turning to Allah at every juncture.

The above is easier said than done. However, if you can maintain such and attitude in such appalling circumstances, your reward, InshAllah will be *Jannah ghaire hisaab* (Paradise without any accountability to Allah).[1]

So even when things are bad for me, I am a still a winner?

Yes. Just imagine it. A Muslim even gets tonnes of rewards from misfortune.

> Allah's Messenger sallallahu alayhe wasallam said, "How wonderful for the believer! All his affairs are full of good, not for anyone, but only for the believer in Allah - If something good happens, he thanks Allah and he is rewarded for that; and if he suffers from some misfortune, he is patient and he is rewarded for it." (Sahih Muslim and Ahmed; also mention in Riyadh as Saaliheen – volume 1)

Story Three

You arrive with your friend in the car park of a supermarket. Your friend refuses to lock the car saying, In the Name of Allah – I put my trust in Allah.

- **As a Muslim, he should not behave foolishly or wrecklessly in his affairs.**
- **I will advise him to first lock his car and then trust in Allah.**

Yes. It is true the whether the car is stolen or not is preordained. However, you are still given freedom of choice in your actions and you must exercise that freedom wisely.

Muhammad sallallahu alayhe wasallam encouraged us trust in Allah but to take all necessary precautions as well.

Story Four

---

[1] Mentioned in Allah's Book as the reward for those who have Sabr.

You are travelling to London from Lahore. On arrival, you discover that your luggage has mistakenly been sent to Los Angeles and will only arrive now, after a week. The other passengers are furious with airport staff.

- **Of course I will put in a formal complaint to the airline, in order that they can look at ways to improve their service;**
- **However, I will remember Allah and peacefully accept that something has happened here outside of my control;**
- **I will stay calm, patient and make do until the luggage arrives;**

Yes. Maybe there was some reason for this event happening. Maybe it contains some hidden benefit, which you will only come to know about later.

Story Five

Somebody's father suddenly dies in a car crash.

- **I will encourage them to have *sabr*, as mentioned before;**
- **I will ask them to remember that all the events of his father's life, good or bad, and including his death, were already ordained to happen by Allah;**
- **He could not extend his father's life by even one second more than had already been decreed;**
- **He should now remember Allah and make sure that he is a *saleh* (righteous) son, upholding his father's good name amongst family and friends.**

Yes. He should remember that *birr* (dutifulness) towards parents even continues after death.

> Malik bin Rabi'ah As Saa'di said, While I was sitting with the Messenger of Allah sallallahu alayhe wasallam, a man from the Ansar came to him and asked, "O Messenger of Allah! After my parents die, is there any type of *birr* that I can perform towards them?" The Prophet sallallahu alayhe wasallam replied: "Yes, there are four qualities to perform:
>
> 1. Pray (to Allah to grant mercy) and invoke (Him) for forgiveness for them;
> 2. Fulfill their promises[1];
> 3. Be generous to their friends;
> 4. Keep relations with the Kindred, which are your kindred through your parents.
>
> This is what remains of the *birr* that you could perform towards them after they die." (Ahmed, Abu Dawood and Ibn Maajah)

---

[1] Including the proper execution of any wills they leave and the settlement of their debts.

Story Six

You are deciding which day to play cricket with your friends, Saturday or Sunday. You all decide on Sunday. Saturday turned out to be a beautiful sunny day. On Sunday, it rained all day. Your match was cancelled and you all stayed in doors. One of your friends says, "If only we had played on Saturday."

- **I will let it be know that this was all by the *Qadar* of Allah;**
- **There was no match on Saturday or Sunday and there was never going to be one;**
- **There are no "ifs" and "buts."**

Yes. We must avoid saying "if" in such situations e.g. "If only I had done such and such" or "if only such and such hadn't happened." This is completely wrong in Islam and opens the door for futile thinking by shaytaan. We, as Muslims, must happily acccept whatever Allah has ordained for us.

> Muslim reports from Abu Hurayrah that Muhammad sallallahu alayhe wasallam said, "A strong believer is better and more beloved to Allah than a weak believer, although both are good. Pay attention to that which benefits you, seek Allah's help, and never feel helpless. If something happens to you, do not say, "if only such and such would have happened." Say instead, "Allah has decreed it, and He does what He wills." Saying "if" only opens the way for *shaytaan*."

Story Seven

Your younger brother tells you in the morning that his "horoscope" in the newspaper is bad today. Later, you are walking with him down the street. You and him both walk under a ladder. Paint from above drips onto both your heads. Your brother complains, "I knew my horoscope was bad for today, I should never have left my house. I knew that walking under ladders brings bad like. I shouldn't have done that also."

- **I will gently scold him and advise him because he has said something very wrong;**
- **I will advise him that ALL good and bad comes ONLY FROM ALLAH;**
- **We do not believe in stupid superstitions, or charms or horoscopes etc.**

Muslims do not believe in good luck or bad luck habits, lucky charms, superstitions, horoscopes, reading tea leaves etc.

All good and bad is from Allah alone.

Test Yourself

95 questions

1. What does the word Islaam mean?
2. Who gave us the name Islaam?
3. What does the word Muslim mean?
4. Why do we not call ourselves "Muhammadan"?
5. Give some examples of doing Allah's Will.
6. Give some examples of acts to avoid that are against Allah's Will.
7. What are the main six beliefs that a Muslim must hold?
8. What are the main five actions that a Muslim must undertake?
9. What is the meaning of the word *tawheed*?
10. Name the three categories of *tawheed* in Arabic and English.
11. What is *Tawheed al Uluhiyyah*?
12. What is *shirk*?
13. Give some examples of *shirk*.
14. Can anybody intercede on your behalf before Allah Ta'aala?
15. Can dead people in their graves help you?
16. What is the meaning of the word *ibaadah*?
17. What is *Tawheed al Rububiyyah*?
18. Explain as far as you can, the meaning of the word *Rab*.
19. Is Allah the *Rab* of Muslims only?
20. Consider the consequences if there were more than one god in the universe.
21. Give some examples of the day to day events that Allah controls.
22. What is the meaning of *Al Asmw wa as Sifaat*?
23. What is the meaning of the word "attribute"?
24. Why are the *Al Asma wa as Sifaat* so important?
25. Is it recommended to learn the *Al Asma wa as Sifaat*? What is the evidence for this?
26. What is the meaning of the word *Ihsa*?

27. How can knowing *Al Asma wa as Sifaat* increase your *eemaan*?
28. How many *Asma wa as Sifaat* does Allah have?
29. We know certain names of Allah. Are there any we do not know about?
30. Is Allah "everywhere'?
31. Can we call Allah by names that He has not used to describe Himself? Give examples.
32. What is the meaning of Al Hannaan and Al Mannaan? Are they acceptable names of Allah?
33. Give an example of a name based upon an action of Allah but not considered amongst His *Asma wa as Sifaat*?
34. What is the meaning of the name Al Maakir? Why is it not acceptable?
35. What is the meaning of the word *taykeef*?
36. Does Allah have hands?
37. If yes to the above, are those hands the same as human hands?
38. Many religions make statues of gods. Does this breach *Tawheed al Asma wa as Sifaat*? Explain your answer.
39. What is the meaning of the word *ta'teel*?
40. Why can't someone call himself Abd ar Rasool?
41. What are the al *malaika*?
42. Why don't *malaika* commit sins?
43. Was Iblees one of the *malaika*? Explain.
44. Name eight *malaika* mentioned in the Qur'aan and *ahadith*.
45. What did *malaika* tell Ibraheem alayhe salaam?
46. What did *malaika* tell Maryam alayhe salaam?
47. Who dictated the words of the Qur'aan to Muhammad sallallahu alayhe was sallam?
48. What did *malaika* do at the Battle of Badr?
49. Who are *Kiraamen Katibeen*?
50. Do *malaika* have wings?
51. Which animal can see *malaika*?
52. What are *al kutub*?
53. Name the four prophets who received Books?
54. Name those books in Arabic and English?
55. Who are the *ehle kitaab*?
56. What changes were made to the previous books?
57. What does the word Qur'aan mean?
58. The Qur'aan has been translated in many languages. Can we call those various translations, "The Qur'aan?" If not, why not?
59. What is the meaning of the word "Furqaan?"
60. What is a *Soorah*? How many of these are there in the Qur'aan?
61. What is the meaning of the word *ayaah*?
62. What is the name of the Arabic of the Qur'aan?
63. What is *Wahy Zaahir*?
64. What is *Wahy Baatin*?
65. What happened in Hira Cave?

66. Name the cousin of Khadija who advised Muhammad sallallahu alayhe was sallam after the event in Hira Cave?
67. What is *Bayt al 'Izza*?
68. What ages was Muhammad sallallahu alayhe was sallam when he received both his first and his last revelations?
69. What is *tanjeem*. What was the possible benefit of *tanjeem*?
70. Who are Allah's *rusul*?
71. How many prophets were there?
72. Who were the first and last prophets?
73. How many prophets are mentioned in the Qur'aan? Name them.
74. What language did the prophets speak in?
75. What kinds of things did the prophets preach? What one message did they preach in particular?
76. Were all the prophets followed by their people? Give examples.
77. What event in the life of Muhammad sallallahu alayhe was sallam happened under a tree?
78. Were the prophets human beings? If yes, how did they perform miracles?
79. Describe some of the good qualities of the prophets.
80. What is *Yawm Al Aakhir*?
81. Give five other names by which *Yawm al Aakhir* is also known?
82. When will *Yawm al Aakhir* take place?
83. How will your parents help you on that Day?
84. Where are *Jannah* and *Jahannam* located?
85. Have *Jannah* and *Jahannam* been created already?
86. How will people enter *Jannah* and *Jahannam*?
87. How are *Jannah* and *Jahannam*?
88. Describe the food of *Jannah* and *Jahannam*?
89. Describe the drink of *Jannah* and *Jahannam*?
90. Are there any people in *Jannah* or *Jahannam* now?
91. What is *Al Qadr*?
92. What are the four aspects of believing in Qadr as identified by Sheikh Ibn Taymiyyah?
93. What is *Lauh al Mahfoodh*?
94. Describe some of those things beyond man's control?
95. What did Muhammad sallallahu alayhe was sallam say about the word "if"?